CONTENTS

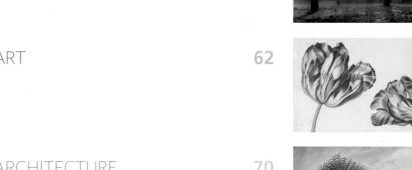

KEW

Like the great River Thames that curves around it, the Royal Botanic Gardens, Kew is always changing. Since it was founded in 1759, it has driven ideas about science and nature and responded to emerging needs of communities around the world. Its landscapes and architecture have mirrored this change and its extraordinary plant collections continue to swell with species newly discovered in forests, mountains, deserts and savannahs.

But not everything changes here. Beauty is constant through the seasons and the years. Visitors experience first-hand the spectacle and wonder of plants in a unique setting. This Guide aims to enrich that experience by exploring some of the stories behind Kew's plants and people, its past and its present.

WELCOME TO KEW

Walking through the gates of the world's leading botanic garden, you discover a place where plants take centre stage. First, you are struck by the scale and beauty of the trees, which ring with bird song. Then paths and sweeping lawns lead you to stunning architecture from every stage in the Gardens' history, built to display rich collections of plants, art and artefacts.

Throughout Kew's historic landscape, enchanting gardens, temples and statues await your arrival. Vistas, glades and dells offer you space to contemplate and to play, while the lofty chambers of the great glasshouses transport you to tropical forests and arid plains. And each time you visit, something will have changed. Flowers open, light alters, seasons pass, gardens mature and the stories you discover about plants and fungi are constantly renewed through festivals and displays.

The Gardens embody the purpose of Kew as the global resource for plant and fungal knowledge. They bring science to life – stimulating curiosity, provoking debate, celebrating beauty and inspiring a love of the natural world.

THE BIRTH OF THE GARDENS

The Gardens were created as 18th-century Britain began to make sense of the world through reason and science. European explorers traversed the globe and brought back exciting new plants. The two adjacent royal estates that were to become the Royal Botanic Gardens showed off these exotic introductions as symbols of wealth and discernment (see Changing Landscape p88). Sir Joseph Banks (below right) joined Captain Cook's famous expedition to the South Seas from 1768 to 1771, and on his return became Kew's first unofficial director, with the aim of creating the finest botanic garden of the age. Kew has been shaped by its plant hunters over the centuries, who have continued to bring the rich variety of the plant kingdom to these Gardens, and expanded its extraordinary collections of objects and botanical art (see Art and Artefacts p64).

QUEST FOR PLANTS

In the 1800s, as British colonies were being founded across the world, Kew's purpose evolved. The hunger for novelty transformed into a quest for plants of economic value (see People Need Plants p22). In 1840, Kew was given by the Crown to the nation. The first official director, Sir William Hooker, developed the Gardens to welcome the public, who came in their thousands to marvel at the plants, displayed outside and in purpose-built glass palaces.

The Palm House and Temperate House are fantastic examples of cutting-edge Victorian technology and Imperial spectacle, and have set the standard for Kew's architecture to this day (see Architecture p70). Sir William Hooker was succeeded as director by his son, Joseph Dalton Hooker. One of the greatest British botanists and plant hunters of the 19th century, he made Kew the hub of a global plant exchange network. For example, seeds of the rubber tree, *Hevea brasiliensis,* were received at Kew in 1876. From these, seedlings were grown, which were then sent to Sri Lanka and Malaysia, becoming the basis for their massive rubber industries.

Joseph Banks (below) was one of the first botanists to use a Wardian case (right) to keep plants alive on long sea voyages.

The Sackler Crossing allows
you to take a sinuous journey
across the Lake and admire
the trees and wildlife.

HORTICULTURAL EXCELLENCE

Kew has offered formal training to gardeners since 1859 and its alumni continue to enrich British and international horticulture. Many have gone on to be great plant collectors themselves, like graduate Ernest Henry Wilson, who introduced plants from China in the early 20th century, including some of the wonderful magnolias that grace the Gardens today (see Magnolias p49). Kew's horticulturists rise to the challenge of creating optimal growing conditions for a vast range of plants and beautiful contemporary displays for over a million visitors a year (see Plants p10).

SCIENCE AND CONSERVATION

While the power and potential of the world's plants are still being revealed, the threat of over-exploitation and environmental change is increasingly apparent. The Gardens are full of plants of economic and medicinal importance including oak, yew, aloe, pepper and bamboo, as well as those of celebrated beauty such as magnolia, tulip, orchid, waterlily and rhododendron. But among them is a growing number of species endangered in the wild (see Back from the Brink p14, and Living Fossils p55). In response, Kew's purpose has evolved again; we now play a pivotal role in an international network of partnerships, as a world leader in plant and fungal science, conservation and plant-based solutions to global environmental challenges.

INSPIRATIONAL GARDENS

Since 2003, the Gardens have been a UNESCO World Heritage Site, recognising the unique combination of plants, architecture, art and landscape and the 260 years of science and ideas. And, Kew is still evolving, through the work of our scientists, horticulturists, educators and many volunteers. Kew reaches out to audiences of every age and origin to delight and inform them, and to inspire them to join us in caring for the natural world and forging a sustainable future for plants and people.

HOW KEW IS FUNDED

The Royal Botanic Gardens, Kew is a non-departmental public body under the National Heritage Act. About one third of Kew's annual running costs are met by the UK government through our sponsoring body, Defra (Department for Environment, Food and Rural Affairs). We generate the rest of our income from entrance fees, membership, commercial activity and philanthropic donations. The commitment of our members and supporters is increasingly important to maintain the Gardens, and to meet the demand for Kew's vital science and conservation expertise around the world.

As you wander through the Gardens look out for some of the exceptional features named after those whose passion has translated into philanthropic support. You can help too, by becoming a member or making a donation – please visit **www.kew.org/support.**

Far left: The new wing of the Herbarium Library Art and Archives building was built to house expanding collections.

Left: Kew's landscape now contains many scientifically important collections and rare species in a beautiful setting.

PLANTS

With horticultural skills and knowledge developed over 250 years, and the latest technologies, we grow 30,000 different kinds of plants, from the tiny critically endangered Rwandan waterlily, *Nymphaea thermarum*, to the huge old *Wisteria sinensis* whose purple racemes cascade over a large pergola in spring.

The glasshouses and gardens of Kew provide carefully managed growing spaces for plants from around the world, creating a living reference library for our scientists and a dynamic landscape in which to display the beauty, wonder and power of this diverse natural kingdom on which all life depends.

The sumptuous flowers of lotus and tropical waterlilies are a star attraction in summer.

PLANTS UNDER GLASS

Kew's glasshouses transport you to other worlds – to the steamy rainforest, the cool arid desert and the bright breezy mountainside. Throughout its history Kew has pioneered techniques to give its plants the growing conditions they need to flourish far from their native lands.

Growing plants under glass presents many challenges. Each species has particular requirements for humidity and temperature, food and light levels. They have come from complex ecosystems – some depend on fungi in the soil to access nutrients, others on insects for pollination or birds to disperse their seeds. They respond to wet and dry seasons, hot and cold. Flowering can be triggered by the length of the day, seed germination by cold or by fire. To grow them successfully, Kew horticulturists must be observant, persistent, skilled and passionate about plants.

The elegant Palm House K 7 is devoted to the rainforest and includes plants that have changed the world. The Para rubber tree, *Hevea brasiliensis*, was the basis of a global industry, just as the African oil palm, *Elaeis guineensis*, is today. Kew research is helping to develop sustainable harvests of these and other products like cocoa and coffee, bananas and vanilla. Important crops like rice, lemon grass and sugar cane are grown around the central pool in the intimate Waterlily House L 6 , home to the stunning Santa Cruz waterlily, *Victoria cruziana*, and the sacred lotus, *Nelumbo nucifera*.

The distinctive arched Davies Alpine House O 8 provides excellent conditions for bulbs and plants from mountain ranges and Arctic shorelines alike, keeping them dry in winter and cool in summer, while the Bonsai House O 8 , gives shade and space to contemplate its fascinating miniaturised trees. The Temperate House F 8 has just undergone a major five-year restoration. Its important collections from the Americas, South Africa, Asia, Australasia and island temperate habitats have just been replanted and include many endangered species being conserved by Kew (see p80).

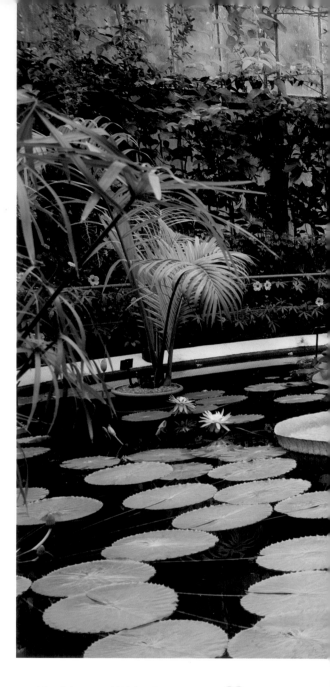

The Princess of Wales Conservatory O 7 displays an astonishing array of plants in ten climatic zones. Here you can find cacti, bromeliads and orchids as well as the titan arum, *Amorphophallus titanum*. Two zones are devoted to carnivorous plants including pitcher plants, *Nepenthes*, and Venus flytraps, *Dionaea muscipula*, which can close on an insect in under half a second.

One of Kew's iconic plants grows in the wet tropical zone. The celebrated giant waterlily, *Victoria amazonica* is grown from seed each year. The leaves first appear as spiny heads but expand rapidly to reach up to 2.8 metres across. The spectacular white flowers open at sunset, filling the air with strong perfume. At Kew, the flowers are hand-pollinated, but in the wild scarab beetles are drawn to feed on the flowers, which then close at night. The next day the flowers turn pink, release their pollen and re-open. The beetles make their escape, brushing pollen onto their sticky bodies as they leave. That night they are drawn to the fragrance of another white flower and pollinate it as they land.

You can find Kew's giant waterlilies in the Waterlily House (above) and in the Princess of Wales Conservatory where the iconic *Victoria amazonica* (left) grows in the central pond.

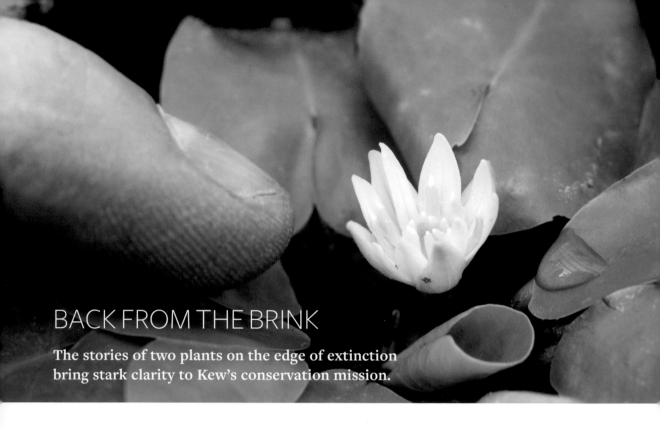

BACK FROM THE BRINK

The stories of two plants on the edge of extinction bring stark clarity to Kew's conservation mission.

THE PYGMY WATERLILY OF RWANDA

The world's smallest waterlily, *Nymphaea thermarum*, was discovered in 1987 growing in the mud around freshwater hot springs and is known from just one location in Mashyuza, in south-west Rwanda. However, it disappeared from there recently due to over-exploitation of the hot spring that fed this fragile habitat. Water was prevented from reaching the surface and the few square metres where this species grew dried out. *Nymphaea thermarum* became extinct in the wild.

Thankfully, Professor Eberhard Fischer, the German botanist who had discovered it, realised that the species was under threat. He had transported a few plants to Bonn Botanic Gardens in Germany, where the horticulturists successfully grew these valuable specimens for more than a decade. However, the pygmy waterlily proved extremely difficult to propagate and it was feared that when these plants reached the end of their natural lives, the species would be lost forever. As a result of a conservation plant exchange with Bonn, a handful of plants came to Kew. After many trials, Kew horticulturists managed to replicate the damp warm conditions of the species' natural habitat and finally coaxed this tiny rarity into flower in 2009.

Once the riddle of its propagation had been solved, *Nymphaea thermarum* was easily cultivated and now more than 50 plants are growing at Kew, some of which can be seen in the Princess of Wales Conservatory and the Waterlily House.

Kew works with partners around the world to build consensus on conservation policy and makes an impact on the ground by offering training in conservation techniques and habitat restoration. Though it is now piped away before it reaches the surface, the hot spring water still flows beneath the native habitat of *Nymphaea thermarum*, and there may be an opportunity in future to restore the site and re-introduce this beautiful species to Rwanda.

CAFÉ MARRON, LOST AND FOUND

Café marron, *Ramosmania rodriguesii*, is a wild coffee relative endemic to Rodrigues, a remote island in the middle of the Indian Ocean that is now part of Mauritius. The small evergreen shrub with glossy leaves and star-shaped white flowers was thought to be extinct. It was last seen in the 1940s and known only from dried specimens and a drawing made in 1877. But in 1984, when shown the drawing by his teacher, a 12-year-old boy insisted that it matched a plant growing near his house. Samples were sent to Kew and we confirmed that he had rediscovered the long-lost café marron. Careful exploration of the island failed to find another specimen and it became clear that this one plant – which was not in the best of health – was the last representative of the species on Earth. Measures were taken to protect the plant on the island but any hope for the future of the species depended on creating new plants.

Kew horticulturists managed to root cuttings sent from Rodrigues but it was another 20 years before they worked out how to produce fruit.

In 2003 the first berry ripened, producing the seeds of new individuals and in 2009 Kew was at last able to send healthy plants back to their island home, where work is ongoing to re-establish a stable population in the wild. At Kew they are grown in the Palm House and the Princess of Wales Conservatory.

The recent history of café marron shows the vulnerability of island floras. Due to their isolation and restricted size, islands are often rich in endemics – plants and animals that occur nowhere else in the world. The natural balance of island ecosystems can be easily upset by the introduction of non-native species. Without any native grazing animals on Rodrigues, its plants had no features to deter the goats that were brought to the island by settlers and grazed café marron to the brink of extinction.

Rodrigues is part of the Republic of Mauritius, where 275 species of plant are critically endangered. Specialist horticultural skills developed at Kew are needed now more than ever to replicate the positive stories of the pygmy waterlily and café marron elsewhere in the world.

Far left: *Nymphaea thermarum*, the world's smallest waterlily, on the giant leaf of the largest, *Victoria amazonica*.

Kew horticulturists managed to root cuttings of the café marron sent from Rodrigues, but it was 20 years before they worked out how to get it to produce fruit with viable seeds for a new generation.

PERFECT ADAPTATIONS

Plants have developed in their natural environments over millions of years and some of their extraordinary adaptations can be seen among plants in the Princess of Wales Conservatory.

Charles Darwin's theory of evolution by natural selection was hugely influenced by the variety of plant adaptations he saw, and he shared his radical ideas with his friend Sir Joseph Hooker, Kew's second official director, as letters in Kew's archive show (see Art and Artefacts p64).

Climbing the column by the stairs in the arid zone of the Princess of Wales Conservatory O7 is a cactus that is adapted to attract bats. The Pitaya or dragon fruit cactus, *Hylocereus polyrhizus* comes from tropical forests of Central America and as far south as Peru. Its buds open at dusk into wide cupped pale flowers that emit a sweet smell and are thought to reflect the sound signals of a hungry echo-locating bat. The bat forces its head into the flower, trying to reach the nectar with its long tongue. In the process its furry body collects large amounts of pollen, which it transfers to the next flower it visits.

Nepenthes robcantleyi has such large pitchers that it is believed its diet might include small mammals and reptiles. It was recognised as a new species in 2011 by Kew specialists, a decade after it was discovered in a single location in the Philippines, where the forest has since been cut down.

GIANT OF THE RAINFOREST

Another night-flowering plant is the titan arum, *Amorphophallus titanum*, from western Sumatra. But its massive flower structure produces neither nectar nor sweet fragrance; on the contrary, it emits the nauseating stench of rotting flesh, an adaptation that attracts insects from great distances through the tropical forest. Every year the single immense mottled leaf of the titan arum grows to the size of a small

tree before dying down again. This annual growth builds up food reserves in its underground tuber until it can produce its huge flower, which rises up to three metres above the ground. The first time it flowered in cultivation was at Kew in 1889, exciting great public interest. In 1926, when it flowered again, the crowds were so large that the police were called to control them. Kew horticulturists have mastered its cultivation and there is almost always a plant in leaf in the wet tropical zone, where the high temperature, shade and humidity recreate the conditions of its natural habitat. The plant can take 20 years to flower from seed and the tubers have been known to weigh up to 90kg, which makes repotting quite a challenge.

Plants have adapted in many ways to find nutrition in inhospitable habitats. Carnivorous and semi-carnivorous plants trap prey such as midges and flies to get nutrients, and their different mechanisms can be seen in two dedicated zones and in the wet tropical zone. Though temperate *Sarracenia* and tropical *Nepenthes* are unrelated, they have evolved to catch their food in the same way and both have pitchers with smooth waxy interior walls. Insects are attracted to the colours and sweet secretions inside the pitchers but once inside they slip, drown and are then digested.

In 1889, Kew became the first place to experience the flowering of the titan arum outside of its native Sumatra.

The Eastern Cape giant cycad in the Palm House arrived at Kew in 1775 and is one of the oldest pot plants in the world.

LIVING HISTORY

Kew has a fine collection of cycads – plants that were widespread on Earth over 250 million years ago, before the dinosaurs and well before the appearance of the flowering plants that now dominate the world's vegetation.

Some of the rarest plants in the Gardens are cycads. With their stout trunks and dense crowns of large whorled pinnate leaves, cycads resemble palms or tree ferns, but they have many unique characteristics. They are long-lived, slow-growing plants that produce male and female cones in the centre of the leaf whorl on separate plants.

One of the cycads at Kew is also a contender for the title of oldest pot-plant in the world. Housed in a large wooden box at the southern end of the Palm House K 7, the Eastern Cape giant cycad, *Encephalartos altensteinii*, arrived at Kew in 1775, sent from South Africa by Kew's first plant hunter, Scottish botanist Francis Masson. In 1819, 44 years after it came to Kew, the Eastern Cape giant cycad produced its first cone. It has not produced another cone since. Now weighing more than a tonne, this venerable plant measures over four metres and leans languidly sideways in a sign of its old age. Though classed as vulnerable in the wild due to the pressures of land clearance, the species is fairly common in South Africa, growing in open shrubland on rocky slopes and in evergreen forest.

You can see many cycads in the Palm House including *Encephalartos ferox*, which produces bright orange-red cones. Pollinating cycads is a tricky business but well worth the effort as they are so endangered in the wild. Kew's 90-year-old male *Encephalartos ferox* hit the headlines when its pollen was extracted using a turkey baster to fertilise a female cycad in Bristol.

In the Temperate House F 8 you can see one of the world's rarest cycads, *Encephalartos woodii*, often called the world's loneliest plant. Only one specimen (a male) was ever found in the wild in South Africa. Kew's specimen is an offset of that original plant and arrived here in 1899.

Cycads are in high demand for the architectural drama they bring to gardens, but to protect wild populations their trade is highly regulated. Kew works internationally, advising governments and assisting the UK and other countries to set priorities for conservation and sustainable use of plant resources, in order to ensure a positive future for plants like the great cycads.

You can see many cycads in the Palm House including *Encephalartos ferox*.

Tough skin and a buoyant husk means the COCONUT can survive in salt water for as long as 2 months, travelling up to 5,000 kilometres on ocean currents. It travels in a dormant state, only activating when it finds fresh water.

ORCHIDS

Kew has one of the best collections of tropical orchids in the world. Many of them are epiphytic – growing in the wild on the trunks and branches of trees. Kew horticulturists aim to mimic their environment in cultivation, providing the right temperatures, humidity and growing places to keep the orchids happy.

You can also see temperate orchids at Kew including bee orchids (*Ophrys*). Some species of *Ophrys* are insect mimics – their flowers can both resemble and smell like female bees. This invites males in, who inadvertently pick up pollen and take it to the next *Ophrys* flower.

The Princess of Wales Conservatory ⓞ7 has two distinct zones devoted to the display of these beautiful plants. A hot, steamy zone features the tropical lowland species with their spectacular showy flowers and adaptations for life in the forest canopy. A second, cooler orchid zone suits the no less attractive species from tropical mountain regions. Many more specimens in Kew's collection are grown in controlled environments in the Tropical Nursery and put on display when they are coming into flower, so visitors can see the immense diversity of this plant family. You'll find perfumed blooms of *Cattleya and Dendrochilum,* strange-looking *Paphiopedilum* slipper orchids, and butterfly-like *Dendrobium*, as well as long branching sprays of small bright flowers of *Oncidium*, tall spikes of the waxy blooms of *Cymbidium*, and the unusual deep-blue and burnt-orange colours of flamboyant *Vanda*. There are also many miniature orchids, with flowers only a few millimetres across. You need to bring your magnifying glass to appreciate their intricate beauty.

Technological advances mean orchids can now be produced commercially on a huge scale, creating an explosion in trade in the last two decades, with plant breeders developing ever more amazing hybrids and cultivars. Moth orchid, *Phalaenopsis,* hybrids are now the most popular house plants in the world. However, many species are endangered in the wild by habitat destruction and over-collecting. Kew, a world leader in the study of orchids, is working to help ensure the conservation and sustainable use of these plants in their natural habitats.

Orchids inspire obsession among scientists and gardeners who have discovered, studied and recorded them for centuries. At a time of orchid mania in Victorian Britain, Charles Darwin published a book on orchids, using his ideas about evolution to explain why they produced such elaborate flowers. The orchid family, Orchidaceae, is one of the largest of all plant families, with around 25,000 species – one in twelve of all flowering plants – distributed across the world, mostly in tropical regions with very high rainfall. Three and a half thousand orchid species have been recorded in Ecuador while only 55 species – all terrestrial – grow naturally in Britain.

Kew celebrates this fascinating plant family at its annual orchid festival in late winter, when thousands of brilliant flowers are put on display.

Vanilla, one of the most popular flavours in the world, comes from the seed capsules of vanilla orchids of the tropical forest. 95% of the world's vanilla 'pods' come from just one species, *Vanilla planifolia*, native to Mexico, which can be seen at Kew growing on a tree in the Palm House.

Each February the Princess of Wales Conservatory is adorned with stunning displays of *Phalaenopsis* and many other orchids.

PEOPLE NEED PLANTS

In Kew's magnificent Palm House, the heat is high, the air is heavy with humidity and sunlight filters through multiple textures and shades of green leaf. These are perfect growing conditions for plants from tropical rainforests, many of which have huge economic and medicinal value.

Rattans are a large group of extremely spiny climbing palms that are a focus of research at Kew, and several species grow in the Palm House K7 . The central part of the long stem of a rattan forms a solid cane, which has a wide range of uses including for furniture making and handicrafts. It has trade value of around US$6.5/£3.9 billion. The longest plant stem ever recorded was a rattan, a species of *Calamus*, that measured nearly 200m in length.

In the Palm House you can see the African oil palm, *Elaeis guineensis*, which gives us the most productive oil crop in the world. Palm oil, extracted from the fruits and seeds, has an enormous range of different uses including fuels, cosmetics and food. However, much of the destruction of forests in some of the most biodiverse areas of the world has been blamed on the extensive cultivation of this species, often in vast monocultures.

MEDICINAL POWERS

The pretty flowers of the rosy periwinkle, *Catharanthus roseus*, catch the shifting light beneath the Palm House trees and it has been a popular bedding plant for a century. But it was also known as a useful folk medicine and modern science found it to be rich in powerful alkaloids. These are now used in treatments

Spices come from many different parts of plants. Pepper is the unripe fruit of a vine, cloves are flower buds, cinnamon is tree bark, nutmeg is a seed.

Powerful treatments for cancer have been developed from the rosy periwinkle. *Catharanthus roseus*, which can be seen in the Palm House.

for cancers, in particular childhood leukaemia and non-Hodgkin's lymphoma. The rosy periwinkle comes from the forests of Madagascar, which have been heavily damaged by human activity, but the plant thrives in disturbed areas so it has survived in its island home. However, its story shows how important it is to preserve areas of rich biodiversity, for there may be other 'miracle drugs' in plants yet to be discovered.

FOOD CROPS WE DEPEND ON

Banana plants are one of the most economically important crops in the world, providing food, shelter and fibre. Thousands of years of domestication have produced the delicious fruit eaten by millions of people. You can see one of the most important dessert bananas, *Musa acuminata* 'Dwarf Cavendish,' growing in the Palm House. It looks very different from wild relatives growing nearby, and other species which have green, silvery, striped or spotted fruits. Edible bananas contain no seed, so they can only be reproduced by separating suckers from the parent plants. This means they lack genetic diversity and are vulnerable to decimation by pests and diseases, as happened in the 1950s when the market-leading banana was virtually wiped out by a single fungus. To prevent the repeat of this kind of disaster, Kew's Millennium Seed Bank is working with the Global Crop Diversity Trust on a ten-year project to protect, collect and prepare seed of the wild relatives of 29 key food crops, including the banana. They can then be used for the development of new varieties that are more resilient to the effects of climate change and more resistant to disease. >>

Far left: The dramatic dry tropics zone display includes plants from arid regions such as species of agave, aloe and cacti.

Left: Pods of *Theobroma cacao* containing cocoa seeds. The flowers and pods grow directly from the trunk – this is known as cauliflory.

In addition to visual wonders like the titan arum giant waterlily, pitcher plants, and many orchids, the Princess of Wales Conservatory ⓞ7 houses plants of great significance to people. Food lovers can see the handsome cacao, *Theobroma cacao*, with its glossy leaves and large seed pods housing the main ingredient for chocolate, and the delicious pineapple *Ananas comosus* – the only edible member of the spiky, highly ornamental bromeliads.

In the extensive dry tropics zone, growing among a spectacular array of cacti, are several species of *Agave*, which have long been used for fabrics, fuel, medicine and alcoholic drinks. These striking, architectural plants come from Mexico and northern South America. There are over 130 species, which have spiny, fleshy leaves adapted for survival in hot arid deserts and mountains. The long, tough leaf fibres of sisal, *Agave sisalana*, are used to make hard-wearing carpets, while the succulent leaf base of *Agave tequilana* is pulped and fermented to make tequila, a strong alcoholic drink.

DEFENDING COASTAL COMMUNITIES

In the wet tropics zone by the central pool, a thicket of slender grey-brown stems rises above the mud. These are actually the stilt roots of the red mangrove, *Rhizophora mangle*, adapted to withstand total submersion in salt water and the action of tidal waves. Of the numerous mangrove species that colonise tropical and subtropical coastlines, red mangrove grows closest to the sea, forming unique ecosystems that have an increasingly important role as rising sea levels threaten tropical coastlines. They act as barriers to coastal erosion, provide natural 'nursery grounds' for many species of fish and other marine life, and trap sediments, allowing development of healthy off-shore coral reefs. As well as protecting coastal communities and providing good fishing, red mangrove is used for house building and canoes, fuel, dye and medicine. Although mangroves can cope with the stress of salt water, it is not a requirement for them, which is why their intriguing complex structures can be seen at Kew.

The Madagascan palm, *Tahina spectabilis,* is so big that each individual adult palm can be counted on satellite images from space. First identified as a new species by Kew botanists in 2008, the palm produces an enormous flower spike, but the whole plant dies after it has finished flowering. In a new population survey in 2017, Kew recorded around 700 individuals, making it critically endangered in the wild. You can see young plants of this amazing species growing in the Palm House.

MONOCOTS
includes irises, lilies, grasses and palms

AGIUS EVOLUTION GARDEN

Located on the site of the old Plant Family Beds, the Agius Evolution Garden N 8 displays plants arranged according to the Plant Tree of Life. This classification is the result of research into plant DNA, revealing how plants are related to each other and how they have evolved over millions of years. A network of paths leads visitors through the planting, and low yew hedges separate the major plant groups, creating a beautiful and enlightening garden.

EARLY DIVERGING EUDICOTS
includes buttercups and poppies

MAGNOLIIDS
includes magnolias, allspice and bay trees

NON FLOWERING PLANTS
includes ferns and conifers

PLANTS IN GARDENS

Kew's mild climate enables plants from all over the temperate world to grow happily outside.

Our horticulturists use an abundance of different aspects – sunny walls, cool dells, woodland margins and watersides – to create the optimal growing environments.

Kew is one of the sunniest places in the British Isles and July and August are the warmest months, with an average maximum temperate of 24°C. While January and February are the coldest months, hard frosts are infrequent. This means Mediterranean plants, including many salvias, grow to perfection in our free-draining soil. Olive and cork oak groves shelter the aromatic shrubs in the Mediterranean Garden (see p32), while south-facing walls protect the more tender salvias and lavenders in the north end of the Gardens. Salvias are important both for horticulture and for medicine and the beautiful salvia border by the Rock Garden O 8 gives Kew scientists a living reference collection to investigate their potential in the treatment of dementia and cancer.

GARDENS WITHIN GARDENS

Some plants are grown according to their physical similarities – extensive brick walls at the northern end of the Gardens provide support for many climbing plants (see p39) – while other collections are grown to reflect their wild habitats in mountains and woodlands (see p30–31) or to display the astounding variety within one family, such as the grasses (see p41).

Throughout its history, the Gardens have been at the vanguard of horticultural fashion, subject not only to the changing demands of science and economics but also to that tyrannical force, which emerged in the Georgian years and remains with us today – good taste. Several of our collections are planted to recall gardens of different periods and cultures, such as the Queen's Garden O 3 , the Duke's Garden P 7 and the Japanese Gateway C 8 , Chokushi-Mon (see p38–39).

WATERING THE PLANTS

One of the biggest challenges is keeping our plants well watered. South-east England is the driest part of the British Isles with only 622mm (24 inches) of rain falling throughout the year. While many Mediterranean plants receive a third of our rainfall in the wild, plants in southern China receive over three times more. Our plants from China, grown in many parts of the Gardens, have played a key role in Kew's project to identify and authenticate the ingredients

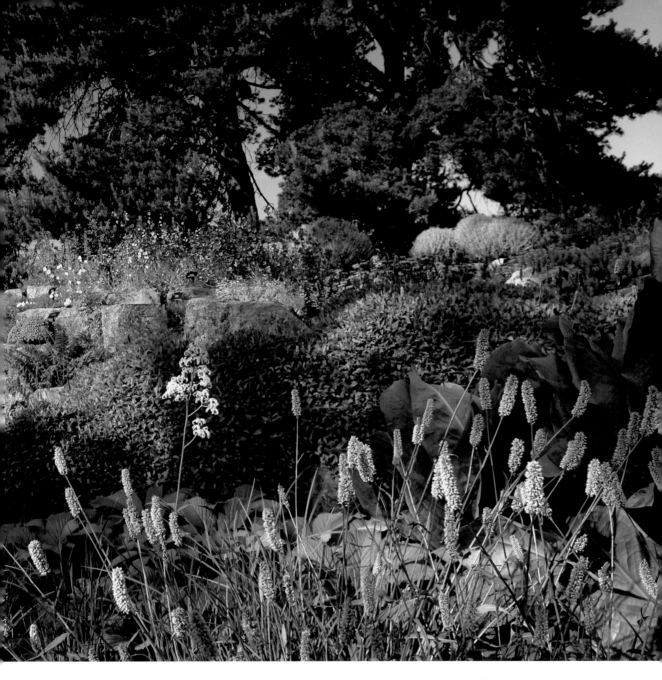

Right plant, right place: Kew aims to give its collections the best possible growing environments.

in traditional Chinese medicine, so the health of the living collections is critical. Huge effort is made to improve our soils so they can hold water and nutrients throughout the drier months. Visitors can see from a specially constructed viewing platform our enormous compost heap E5 , where all the grass cuttings, tree and flower prunings are shredded and turned in enormous piles to produce the mulch which is then redistributed on our shrub and flower beds.

HABITAT GARDENS

Mountains make up a quarter of the global landmass and mountain flora is as diverse as it is beautiful.

The Rock Garden and Woodland Garden, together with the Davies Alpine House 08 recall the habitats of temperate mountains, from deciduous forest to rocky outcrop. Here we grow around 4,000 herbaceous plants and shrubs, adapted to survive extreme weather conditions, perilous cliffs and shady clefts. The Alpine Nursery, behind the scenes, is home to another 3,000 plants, grown in pots, including National Collections of tulips and juno irises. These are displayed in the Davies Alpine House when in full flower.

LIFE ON THE EDGE

Alpines are plants that live at high altitudes where trees cannot survive. They may look delicate but they are tough and fascinating for the many different ways they have adapted to thrive in their harsh environments. They often have dramatic flower displays, out of proportion to their diminutive size, to attract insect pollinators that are fewer in number in the high mountains. Another common survival strategy is a mat of hairs on leaf surfaces, providing protection from both the wind and the sun, which is more intense in the cleaner, thinner air.

First built in 1882 using limestone rock to mimic a Pyrenean mountain valley, complete with cascades and meandering streams, the Rock Garden is now constructed entirely of West Sussex sandstone, which supports a wider range of plants. It is planted in six geographic regions and while it reaches its flowering peak in May there are blooms to admire all year, right through to the miraculous early snowdrops from the Taurus mountain range in Turkey, *Galanthus elwesii*, which emerge just before Christmas.

The delicate blooms of trout lilies and dog's tooth violets, *Erythronium*, light up the Woodland Garden in spring.

JEWELS OF THE FOREST FLOOR

The high point of the Woodland Garden is in March and April. The warming sun reaches the forest floor, which bursts into flower before the trees come into full leaf. Many herbaceous woodlanders have developed bulbs or other underground storage organs to survive the dry and shade of summer. One such is the curious yellow wake robin (*Trillium luteum*), from the forests of the Appalachian Mountains of North America, whose three twisting petals sit on a platform of three mottled leaves. *Trillium* belong to the family Melanthiaceae, which have huge amounts of DNA in their cells. They are attracting keen interest from Kew's geneticists who are trying to understand the role that DNA plays in the way plants evolve.

In late spring and early summer, Himalayan blue poppies (*Meconopsis*) put on a stunning show in the Woodland Garden.

Rich scents of aromatic shrubs such as lavender (above) fill the air in the Mediterranean Garden.

MEDITERRANEAN DIVERSITY

Five regions around the world share the distinctive climate that we call 'Mediterranean', with dry summers, mild moist winters and only sporadic frost. These rocky coastal areas in California, Chile, South Africa, south-west Australia and the Mediterranean Basin are floral treasure-chests, home to 20% of the world's plant life – almost 50,000 species – though they cover less than 2% of its landmass.

Kew's Mediterranean Garden H7 echoes the wild hillsides of southern Spain and the Greek islands. Many plants from the region have small evergreen leaves with leathery cuticles, to protect them from the hot sun and drying winds. A range of species contain aromatic chemicals to deter herbivores like goats and rabbits. On warm days rich scents from these pretty shrubs such as lavender, *Lavandula*, and rock rose, *Cistus*, rise to the Tuscan portico of King William's Temple, which sits on a low mound above the garden. From here the view is framed by groves of trees that have played key roles in Mediterranean civilisations including the cork oak, *Quercus suber*, whose rugged thick grey bark is harvested for cork bottle stoppers for the wine industry; the stone pine, *Pinus pinea*, source of pine nuts – a flavoursome ingredient of the region's cuisine, and the olive tree, *Olea europaea*, whose small black fruits are rich in oil.

CONSERVING ISLAND FLORA

Kew is working with six conservation organisations on the main Mediterranean islands – Sicily, Sardinia, Cyprus, Corsica, Crete and Mallorca – to ensure the survival of their endangered plants.

As with all Kew's scientific collections, the Mediterranean Garden aims to showcase only 'natural sourced' material – plants grown from seed collected in the wild, so that this beautiful place continues to be the most magnificent living reference library in the world.

DESIGNED GARDENS

Kew Gardens has changed throughout its history, reflecting the development of its purpose and changing ideas about how plants should be displayed.

While the major influences are from the 18th and 19th centuries, garden styles of other periods and cultures can be found in secluded corners.

The Queen's Garden 03 complements Kew Palace, drawing on 17th-century fashions in plants and garden architecture. Most of the plants seen here are those which were grown in Britain in the 1600s and earlier. The geometric parterre with its clipped box and fountain, the pleached hornbeam alley, mount and statues were all elements of the gardens of grand houses of the period. Scholars and physicians of the time published 'herbals' – compendia of plant lore and botanical cures, and quotes from these books are included on plant labels in the charming Nosegay Garden. While many appear archaic and comical, they were often grounded in fact. It was said that common sage, *Salvia officinalis*, 'quickeneth the senses and memory' and, 400 years on, Kew scientists are investigating it as a treatment for Alzheimer's disease. >>

The Great Broad Walk Borders are the longest double herbaceous borders in the country at around 320 metres long. Planted for summer colour, they also offer plenty of interest in spring and autumn too.

Kew horticulturists work through the seasons to ensure world-class displays.

EVOKING THE EAST

An even earlier garden style lies at the southern end of the estate, where late 16th-century Japan is evoked by small tea gardens of Peace, Activity and Harmony enclosing a symbolic miniature landscape, all designed by Professor Fukuhara of Osaka University.

On a raised mound at its centre is Chokushi-Mon, a replica of the Gateway of the Imperial Messenger in Kyoto C8 . The finest example of a traditional Japanese building in Europe, it came to Kew after it was constructed for the 1910 Japan-British Exhibition in London.

Look out for beautiful flowering cherries here in spring, anemones and rhododendrons in summer and stunning leaf colours in autumn.

THE GREAT BROAD WALK BORDERS

Planted over the course of 2015, the Great Broad Walk Borders O5 first flowered in 2016 to great acclaim. At over 320 metres long they are thought to be the longest double herbaceous borders in the country, possibly the world! You'll find beautiful spring bulbs here including alliums, daffodils and tulips, and plenty of autumn interest too, but these borders are at their peak in the summer months. They contain around 30,000 plants within eight large circular beds, each of which has a theme, showing off different types of plants or plant families.

From spectacular cultivars to wild species used in research at Kew, there is plenty to discover along the borders, and this is an ideal spot to get inspiration for your own garden. Look out for swathes of the golden yellow *Rudbeckia fulgida* var. *deamii*, *Geranium* 'Orion', salvias, lilies, spires of *Verbascum* and *Phlomis*, and unusual additions such as *Berkheya purpurea* – a daisy species from South Africa. Each bed has a plant list for you to view, while the full plant list and border designs are available in the book *The Great Broad Walk Borders* by Richard Wilford, at the Victoria Plaza shop.

ENGLISH FLOWER GARDEN

The walled Duke's Garden P7 has the more intimate atmosphere of a traditional 20th-century English flower garden. Its extensive borders are filled with bulbs and herbaceous perennials set off by large, manicured lawns while winter interest comes from fragrant shrubs and the gnarled trunk of the Persian ironwood, *Parrotia persica*, with its fascinating peeling bark. More contemporary is the Gravel Garden Q7, developed in the late 20th century in response to growing awareness about climate change. It displays attractive drought-tolerant plants that require minimal watering during summer, such as grasses, euphorbias and Mediterranean herbs.

The northern end of the Gardens has a wealth of mellow brick walls and other structures offering wonderful displays of climbing plants. Species from many different plant families have evolved to climb, using other trees and shrubs, rocks and cliffs, to reach sunlight without having to invest their energy into developing self-supporting structures. Charles Darwin's work on climbing plants helped to advance his theory of evolution by natural selection.

WISTERIAS AND ROSES

Wisterias and roses are among those climbers that develop woody frameworks that persist throughout their winter dormancy. Generations of horticulturists have mastered their cultivation and pruning to achieve the greatest spectacle.

Wisterias are powerful vines from China and North America, which climb by twining their stems around any adjacent support. Kew's huge old *Wisteria sinensis* P6, looks its best in April when its purple racemes cascade over an old iron pergola. You can sit inside this plant, breathing in its scent and admiring the fact it is nearly 200 years old. One of the first in Europe, it was propagated from a plant sent in 1816 from a Cantonese merchant.

Though the rose is seen as an iconic English plant, it has been cultivated in China for thousands of years, and in Europe since Roman times. The 120-metre-long Rose Pergola O8 supports 26 cultivars of rose, which climb using thorns as grappling irons. They have been chosen for their profusion and length of flowering and reach their peak in June creating a fragrant tunnel of colour.

GRASSES

When grown en masse, the beauty and diversity of grasses is revealed. The areas at Kew devoted exclusively to this important plant family are striking and atmospheric.

The Bamboo Garden H3 was created in 1892 in a secluded dell near the river, fuelling a craze among gardeners, who still delight in their elegant coloured stems, and leaves whispering of far-away places. It was not until recent decades that other grasses have become as popular in horticulture and the Grass Garden P8 shows off their elemental grace. Situated just north of the Davies Alpine House, it is designed to display a multitude of textures and colours, changing through the seasons from the spikey green shoots of early spring to the bleached feathery seedheads that catch the winter sun.

Grasslands cover a fifth of the world's land and are absent only in parts of Greenland and Antarctica. They are intertwined with mankind's development, providing us with grains such as wheat, barley and maize, pasture for our livestock and shelter. Grasses are used for biofuel, building materials, paper and alcoholic drinks. The Grass Garden shows tropical and temperate cereal cultivars, while in the Waterlily House and Palm House you can see tropical grasses such as rice, *Oryza sativa*, and sugar cane, *Saccharum officinarum*, which produces around 75% of the world's sugar supply.

HIGHLY EVOLVED

Grasses are wind-pollinated, so they have not evolved to produce showy flowers or strong scents to persuade insects or other creatures to do the work. They have hollow stems and grow from the plant base, rather than the tip, so that when they are grazed by herbivores they can regenerate – this is why cutting your lawn does not kill the grass. In spite of these adaptations, some grasses, including bamboos, are threatened in their wild habitats. Kew scientists working on the remote South Atlantic island of St Helena, a UK Overseas Territory, recently discovered a previously unnamed species of wavy hair grass. The conservation of St Helena Grass, *Eragrostis episcopulus*, is important, as the sites where it grows

are rich in other rare plants. By retreating to remote cliffs and rocky outcrops, these pockets of diversity – found nowhere else in the world – have survived competition from non-native plant invaders and rabbits introduced by settlers. As a first step in the long-term conservation of the grass, seeds have been collected and stored in Kew's Millennium Seed Bank and the grass is now being grown in nurseries on St Helena and at Kew.

There are around 1,000 species of bamboo, growing in many different climates from cold mountain regions to warm, tropical areas, all over the world from China, Japan and the Himalaya to the Americas. They range from low-growing species to giant varieties that reach 35 metres tall and they are used to make scaffolding, house-frames, musical instruments and textiles.

The Grass Garden is planted like a traditional herbaceous border, centred on a rectangular 'pool'. This central area features the Joanna Garston Grass Collection and is planted with two ecologically important British native species – blue moor grass, *Sesleria caerulea*, and purple moor grass, *Molinia caerulea* subsp *caerulea* 'Paul Petersen'.

TREES

Trees have been at heart of the Royal Botanic Gardens, Kew since its earliest days. Several great specimens have witnessed its entire history, through agricultural and industrial revolution, through world wars, the discovery of penicillin and DNA to the turn of the Millennium. In today's technology-driven, hyper-connected world new tree species are still being discovered and the value of the world's forests climbs ever higher, as we understand more clearly their contribution to the environment, climate stability, biodiversity and humanity.

Kew's hardy trees and shrubs combine in a living landscape that changes through the seasons. To explore them is to gain an insight into the beauty and diversity of forests around the globe and also, through the Natural Areas, to connect with a very local woodland.

THE ARBORETUM

Kew's 14,000 magnificent trees are planted throughout the Gardens, representing over 2,000 species and varieties.

This great scientific collection provides grand vistas, glades of mixed woodland, copses of trees from the same plant family and specimens of heritage status. Interest weaves through the changing seasons, from dramatic structures laid bare by winter to the exquisite blooms of magnolias (see p48) and dogwoods in spring, and the mass displays of autumn colour by the maples, oaks and hickories.

Princess Augusta founded the Gardens in 1759 with five acres of trees planted according to the botanical understanding of the time. Within 15 years, the collection had swollen to nearly 800 species, including rarities like the monkey puzzle, *Araucaria araucana* P5, from Chile and the maidenhair tree, *Ginkgo biloba* (see p49). The botanic gardens later incorporated the adjoining royal estate, which had its own unusual trees such as the cedar of Lebanon, *Cedrus libani*, sweet chestnut, *Castanea sativa*, the tulip tree, *Liriodendron tulipifera,* and red oak, *Quercus rubra* (see p50). A wonderful specimen of the North American black walnut, *Juglans nigra*, known to have been planted in the 1730s, grows in the Woodland Garden N8.

Today's Arboretum – a 19th-century term derived from Latin and literally meaning 'a place with trees' – was developed by Sir William Hooker, who was director of the Gardens from 1840 when it was given to the nation by the Crown. In 1844 he challenged landscape designer William Andrews Nesfield to come up with a design for a scientific and educational tree collection that had a 'park-like character' (see Living History, p90).

The Great Pagoda and Syon Vistas are features from this period and, with Cedar Vista, planted in 1871, form a monumental triangle of great avenues through the Arboretum, connecting the Palm House, the Pagoda and the River Thames at Syon House. Cedar Vista passes through the Woodland Glades E5, which are planted with collections of trees and shrubs from Kew expeditions, while Syon Vista is a

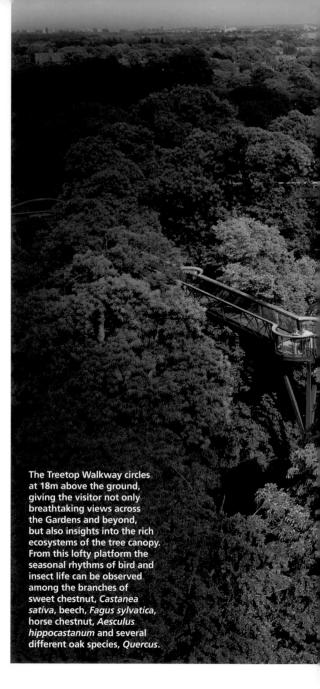

The Treetop Walkway circles at 18m above the ground, giving the visitor not only breathtaking views across the Gardens and beyond, but also insights into the rich ecosystems of the tree canopy. From this lofty platform the seasonal rhythms of bird and insect life can be observed among the branches of sweet chestnut, *Castanea sativa*, beech, *Fagus sylvatica*, horse chestnut, *Aesculus hippocastanum* and several different oak species, *Quercus*.

stately progression of holm oaks, *Quercus ilex*. The original trees forming Nesfield's Pagoda Vista have been replaced by the North American pin oak, *Quercus palustris*, sweet gum, *Liquidambar styraciflua*, and Turkish hazel, *Corylus colurna*, which are suited to avenue planting and Kew's dry soil, and produce fiery displays in autumn.

Sir William Hooker's son, Sir Joseph Hooker, continued to develop the Arboretum, planting many trees and shrubs in groups according to genera for comparison and ease of research. Holly Walk H6

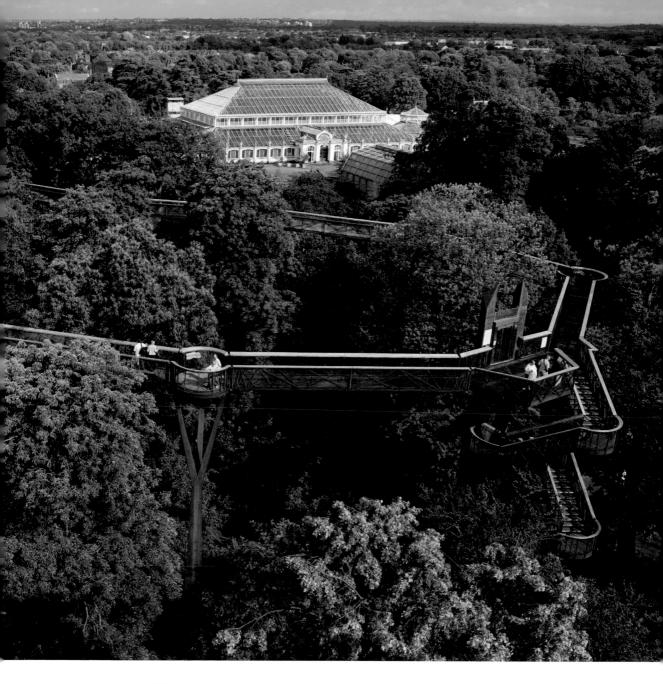

and the Berberis Dell I 9 , laid out in the 1870s, show the wonderful variety of foliage, form and fruit of holly, *Ilex*, and barberry, *Berberis*, while the Redwood Grove D 5 , planted a decade earlier on the fringe of the Pinetum D 4 , is now home to Kew's tallest tree (see Conifers p52).

MANAGING THE ARBORETUM

Today, Kew's Arboretum is managed by a permanent team of tree specialists, which works year-round to monitor and maintain the health and structural integrity of more than 14,000 trees. Highly skilled climbers make regular inspections, reaching the most inaccessible canopies using ropes and pulleys, while another team specialises in planting, ensuring that young trees get the best possible start in the Gardens.

Older trees, dating from the original royal estates or the inception of the Arboretum receive particular care. The soil around their roots is injected with a mixture of air and beneficial fungi to reduce compaction, allow them to absorb more nutrients, and increase their lifespan.

FOUR SEASONS THROUGH KEW'S TREES

In every month, Kew's trees guarantee spectacle and beauty. Make sure you visit in each season to see some of the world's botanical highlights.

SPRING

Spring comes early to the Gardens with the acid-yellow haze of the Cornelian cherry, *Cornus mas*, and the fragrant spidery flowers of the witch hazels, *Hamamelis*, around King William's Temple I 7. Exquisite waxy blooms of *Magnolia* (see p49) can be seen from late March onwards. One of the biggest draws of the season are the cherries. Cherries have been venerated in Japan for 5,000 years and many ornamental varieties have been developed from the wild species. Cherry Walk stretches from the Rose Garden by the Palm House to the Great Pagoda and showcases 11 magnificent cultivars of ornamental cherry trees from Japan, producing clouds of blossom in spring. It's also worth looking out for the handkerchief tree, *Davidia involucrata*, with its showy white bracts that flutter in the cool May winds. There are fine specimens near the Waterlily House L6 and in the Woodland Garden N8.

SUMMER

May brings the sumptuous flowers of several *Paulownia* species, from China and Eastern Asia. Panicles of tubular purple and yellow flowers emerge above the huge downy leaves of the empress tree from Japan, *Paulownia tomentosa* E5, which is traditionally planted to mark the birth of a baby girl. Early summer sees a marvellous floral display from North America's indian been tree, *Catalpa bignonioides* H7, and the Chinese fringe tree, *Chionanthus retusus* H7, and through the hot months of July and August, light and shade play through verdant canopies of leaves.

AUTUMN

Lighting the touch paper of autumn is American ash, *Fraxinus americana* J6, whose dome of willowly foliage is the first in the Gardens to change colour, starting with a stealthy blush of purple that becomes a wild display of red, yellow and orange. It is followed by fiery autumn leaves throughout the Gardens. The flame is carried by an unusually large specimen of *Cotinus obovatus* near Victoria Plaza J9, the Italian maple, *Acer opalus*, towards White Peaks M5, and in the Arboretum by the oak and walnut family collections. The conflagration reaches a peak in the blazing red leaves of the maples, *Acer* G9, to the east of the Temperate House and the brilliant yellow of the hickory, *Carya* D10, towards Lion Gate. South of the Temperate House you will find fruitful plantings of wild crab apples, *Malus*, pear, *Pyrus*, and rowans, *Sorbus,* laden with glistening berries in colours ranging from pinks to oranges and bright reds.

WINTER

The deciduous trees shed their leaves in carpets of colour and a different beauty is revealed in their structures, while low winter sun bounces from the silver flanks of many evergreen species of gum, *Eucalyptus*, planted near White Peaks M4 . Light shines through the slivers of orange tissue that peels from the paperbark maple, *Acer griseum*, north of the Princess of Wales Conservatory and salmon-coloured ribbons of the Japanese birch, *Betula ermanni* N8 before the whole extraordinary cycle begins again.

65% of flowering plants are pollinated by insects. The most important insect pollinators are the world's 20,000 bee species, which collect nectar for energy and pollen for protein. Bee flowers are mostly yellow or blue (as bees can't detect red).

Each season offers sensory delight as trees flower, change colour and then reveal their structural forms.

MAGNOLIAS

Magnolias are adored for their velvet buds, extravagant blooms, handsome foliage and intense fragrance. With over 250 magnolias planted around the Gardens, springtime at Kew is synonymous with this wonderful genus.

There are around 300 species of these flowering trees and shrubs, native to East Asia and the Americas. Though there are tropical species, Kew's collection comes entirely from temperate regions. The first magnolia ever seen in Britain was the swamp bay magnolia, *Magnolia virginiana,* from North America, which was sent to Henry Compton, Bishop of London, in 1687.

An early addition to the Gardens at Kew was a cucumber tree, *Magnolia acuminata,* planted in the late 1700s and still growing on the Orangery Lawn. It does not produce the floral spectacle of its relatives, with small green-yellow flowers obscured by long pointed leaves, but it is striking for its mini cucumber-like fruits which turn from green to bright pink in autumn before ripening to dark-red and splitting to release their red fruit.

Half-a-century after the North American species arrived came the first species from Asia, equalling if not surpassing their western cousins. Sir Joseph Banks, Kew's unofficial first director, introduced the Chinese lily tree, *Magnolia denudata*, in 1780. By then it had been cultivated in China for at least a thousand years and valued as a symbol of candour and purity.

Most prolific of magnolia collectors was Ernest Henry Wilson, who had been a student gardener at Kew before embarking on his celebrated career as a plant hunter. In the early 20th century he introduced eight new species of magnolia that are still widely grown today and grace Kew's collections, including one which bears his name, *Magnolia wilsonii*.

In 1868 Sir Joseph Hooker, Kew's second official director, introduced an exquisite Himalayan species to Britain. Campbell's magnolia, *Magnolia campbellii*, is one of the earliest of Kew's magnolias to flower, producing large blooms between February and April.

Magnolias are thought to have evolved early in the lineage of flowering plants. As far back as 65 million years ago they grew in vast forests together with sweet gum, *Liquidambar*, maidenhair tree, *Gingko*, and tulip tree, *Liriodendron*. Magnolias evolved even before bees and their flowers are extremely robust in order to cope with the weight of their beetle pollinators. The beetles are attracted by the fragrance, and the white, pink or red colour of their flowers, which signal plenteous pollen – a rich food source.

Kew botanists and horticulturists continue to enrich botanical collections worldwide, replenishing stock with seed gathered under license from populations in the wild. Magnolia seeds brought back from the forests of Hokkaido, Japan, in 1998 have grown into trees that only now are beginning to flower in the Gardens.

Left: Magnolias are renowned for their showy, often fragrant flowers. In deciduous species, such as *M. x loebneri* 'Leonard Messel', these often open long before the leaves.

THE MIGHTY OAK AND ITS RELATIVES

The oak family, Fagaceae, provides Kew Gardens with some of its most impressive trees, including the largest, oldest and – perhaps – most curious.

The chestnut-leaved oak, *Quercus castaneifolia* M6 is the largest tree in the Gardens. Coming from the Caucasus and Iran, no finer example of this species is known in the world. It is widely acknowledged to be one of the biggest trees in Britain, measuring over 30m tall and 30m wide. Planted in 1846, it has reached its great size in just under 170 years, making it the fastest growing tree in the Gardens.

The chestnut-leaved oak is so called because its leaves are likened to those of Kew's oldest planted tree, a sweet chestnut, *Castanea sativa*. The gnarled and twisting specimen near the Mediterranean Garden 16 exhibits features that are rarely seen in its native habitat, the dense chestnut forests of southern Europe. The watchful care of generations of Kew arboriculturists has given this and other nearby trees the space and long life to develop such intriguing character. Also belonging to the oak family, the sweet chestnut is thought to have been introduced to Britain by the Romans and it is an important element of ancient coppiced woodland in southern England.

A rival for the title of oldest tree also pre-dates Princess Augusta's botanical garden. Near the head of the Lake 16 and not far from a line of old sweet chestnuts, stands an immense English oak, *Quercus robur*. It may have been planted over 285 years ago when the famous landscape designer Charles Bridgeman worked on this area when it was part of the Richmond estate belonging to George II and Queen Caroline (see Changing Landscape p88).

The title of 'most curious' tree at Kew may go to another member of the oak family – the weeping beech, *Fagus sylvatica* 'Pendula', which was planted in 1846 between the Broad Walk and the Ice House N7. Where its sinuous boughs have dived back to the ground, they have put out roots and new trunks have sprung up. Over time, repeated layering has created a vast complex of smooth grey limbs, only revealed when its magnificent display of autumn leaves is shed and the low light of the winter sun penetrates its shady cavern.

It is no accident that so many oaks are planted in the Gardens. There are around 600 species of oak worldwide and they are revered for their strong timber, long life and ecological value. Kew's oak collection ranges along the riverside, and many huge oaks from North America, such as the northern red oak, *Quercus rubra*, can be found as specimen plantings, setting the Gardens ablaze with their spectacular red leaves in autumn.

In one summer a large oak may use up to 40,000 litres of water, releasing it into the atmosphere through 700,000 leaves. It produces enough oxygen in a year for ten people.

CONIFERS

As specimen trees, conifers make powerful statements. At Kew you can find them massed in the Pinetum where the wealth of form and colour within this ancient and enigmatic group of plants becomes apparent.

Only three conifers are native to Britain – the Scots pine, *Pinus sylvestris*, yew, *Taxus baccata*, and juniper, *Juniperus communis*. As travel became more commonplace in the 18th century, owners of the great estates craved the exotic drama brought to the landscape by the cypress of Italy, the cedar of the Levant and the white pine of North America. The early 19th century brought great numbers of new conifer species to the UK and one conifer from Kew's original five acre arboretum survives – the Corsican pine, *Pinus nigra*, planted in 1814 and still standing near Elizabeth Gate.

Kew's second official director Sir Joseph Hooker was fascinated by conifers, both for their beauty and their economic value. In the 1860s he developed the Pinetum C4 on the south side of Kew's Lake. Wandering through the groves, the extraordinary diversity of cone colours and shapes can be seen amongst the dark needle-like foliage, from the spiky spiralled candles of the pines to the bright open 'berries' of the yew. Conifers are pollinated by the wind, their lightweight pollen grains borne through the air to fertilize female cones of the same species, which then produce seed.

Growing in the Gardens are several grand specimens of stone pine, *Pinus pinea,* with its distinctive umbrella-like structure. Highly valued for its edible seeds known as 'pine nuts', it has been cultivated in Europe for almost 2,000 years.

Conifers appeared over 300 million years ago – indeed, their fossilized remains help scientists trace the geological history of the Earth. Over the millennia they have struggled to compete with the flowering trees that evolved later. While there are believed to be between 60,000 and 80,000 tree species globally, there are just 615 species of conifer, 200 of which occur in tropical forests and savannahs.

Over a third of conifers are now under threat, through habitat destruction and over-exploitation. World knowledge of this fascinating plant group has been dramatically improved with the work of Kew experts who produced, in collaboration with the University of Oxford, the first ever *Atlas of the World's Conifers*. With descriptions and maps of the distribution of each of the 615 known species of conifer, it includes recent discoveries like the amazing Wollemi pine, *Wollemia nobilis* (see p55).

One of the most atmospheric places in the Arboretum is the towering Redwood Grove, planted in the 1860s, where giant redwoods, *Sequoiadendron giganteum,* stand in solemn majesty with coastal redwoods, *Sequoia sempervirens*. Among them is Kew's tallest tree, a coastal redwood, which at nearly 40m is the height of a 13-storey building. A tree of the same species growing in Redwood National Park, California, is believed to be the world's tallest living organism, reaching nearly three times higher than Kew's giant, at 115m high.

We urgently need to find ways to reduce the amount of carbon dioxide in the atmosphere to help reduce the effects of climate change. Trees that decorate our urban landscapes play an important role in taking potentially harmful carbon out of the air. At Kew Gardens scientists estimate that its 14,000 trees 'draw down' approximately 8.6 tonnes of carbon dioxide out of London's air every year.

The atmospheric Redwood Grove, off Cedar Vista, is home to Kew's tallest tree.

The ancient *Ginkgo* at Kew was originally planted next to Princess Augusta's 'Great Stove' glasshouse – now long gone. It is now a Champion Tree – meaning it is the largest of its kind in the country.

THE LIVING FOSSILS

The longevity, beauty and symbolic power of two ancient tree species has assured their future through cultivation.

THE NOBLE PINE

In 1994 the discovery of a conifer in a remote canyon in south-east Australia sent shock-waves through the botanical world. Similar trees were known from the fossil record, but were thought to have become extinct millions of years ago. It became clear that this was a species new to science. It was named *Wollemia nobilis*, the Wollemi pine, after the region where it was found and the man who discovered it, David Noble. The remaining natural populations – around 100 mature trees in all – grow in deep sandstone gorges, the tallest being 40m high and perhaps 1,000 years old.

Kew has helped to secure the future of this species by conducting hardiness trials over several years, proving that young trees coped well with the UK climate. The Wollemi pine has become prized by gardeners, and propagated plants are being sold around the world, raising money to help conserve the wild populations. Kew's Wollemi pines can be found on the Orangery Lawn O5, in a group near the Treetop Walkway F7, and on the Lake islands F3, where a 6m-high specimen is the largest in the UK. The trees have matured rapidly, and are already producing seed, which has been used to grow Kew's collection. Unlike their close relative the monkey puzzle, *Araucaria araucana*, single trees develop numerous trunks with characteristic knobbly dark-brown bark that resembles bubbling chocolate. The tree is evergreen, but its pendulous frond-like foliage changes from fresh apple-green to bluish as it ages and in colder months is tinged with bronze.

TRUE SURVIVOR

Another tree that time forgot is the maidenhair tree, *Ginkgo biloba*. It is the only surviving member of an ancient group of plants that were widespread at the same time as the dinosaurs, 180–200 million years ago. But *Ginkgo* barely survived the ice ages in scattered pockets of eastern and southern China. Like the Wollemi pine, its best hope for a future was mankind. Thankfully, early modern people found medicinal and cultural uses for it. Its distinctive leaves and great longevity have brought it a powerful symbolic role and many ancient specimens – up to 3,500 years old – grace the grounds of Buddhist temples.

Though endangered in the wild, the *Ginkgo* has re-colonised the world through the activities of people. It came to Europe from Japan around 1730 and arrived in North America soon after. Its resistance to disease and pollution make it a valued addition to the contemporary urban landscape and it is now one of the most common street trees in New York City. The extracts of its leaves are being investigated in advanced biomedical research, informed by Kew's detailed studies of its traditional medicinal uses.

Kew has many examples of this beautiful tree. Our oldest *Ginkgo biloba* is thought to have been planted around 1762 in the original botanic garden of Princess Augusta P6.

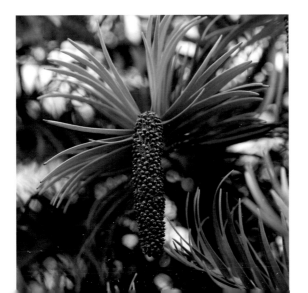

The distinctive seed-bearing cones of the Wollemi pine can be observed all year round in the UK but male cones mature in late September and early October.

NATURAL AREAS AT KEW

While Kew is best known for its work with plants from across the globe, there is a quiet enclave devoted exclusively to habitats of south-east England

The Natural Areas B2, at the south-western end of the Arboretum, are a mosaic of meadow and woodland beside the River Thames. They are managed to encourage native flora and fauna. A network of sinuous paths leads the visitor into a wild, romantic place quite different from the stately vistas and designed landscapes that surround it.

These 15 hectares of sylvan beauty were given to Kew by Queen Victoria in 1898, on the condition that they remained in their natural state. The gift included Queen Charlotte's Cottage, built in the 1760s in a woodland glade (see Changing Landscape p88).

At the time of Queen Victoria's gift, it was thought that conservation could be achieved simply by fencing off areas and leaving them to natural processes without any interference. The intervening century has seen a resurgence of traditional cycles of woodland and meadow management, as their importance to wildlife and diversity has been rediscovered. Kew has embraced this approach: the removal of non-native trees and shrubs, judicious mowing, the introduction of coppicing and the

In spring the woodland floor around Queen Charlotte's Cottage becomes a sea of blue thanks to the native bluebell, *Hyacinthoides non-scripta*. Britain is the northern limit of the bluebell's natural range and has nearly half the world's bluebell population. A large colony can indicate that a wood is ancient and likely to be rich in other rarer species.

protection of small wetland areas all play a part in the ongoing development of this precious retreat, while standing dead trees are retained as habitats for invertebrates, fungi, bats and birds.

The tree community is made up of a mix of mature native broadleaf species such as oak, *Quercus robur*, hornbeam, *Carpinus betulus*, beech, *Fagus sylvatica*, alder, *Alnus glutinosa*, and ash, *Fraxinus excelsior*, with naturalised species of horse chestnut, *Aesculus hippocastanum,* and sweet chestnut, *Castanea sativa*. The understorey has been dominated by yew, *Taxus baccata*, and holly, *Ilex aquifolium*, but these evergreens are being thinned in favour of plants that cast less shade, such as mountain ash, *Sorbus aucuparia*, hawthorn, *Crataegus monogyna*, and spindle, *Euonymus europaea*. You can see many of these species and learn more about them on the Woodland Walk – a boardwalk trail through a previously hidden glade C1 .

Apart from providing beautiful and peaceful places, woodlands have many benefits including making us more resilient to climate change, conserving biodiversity, contributing to a sustainable green economy and improving our health and well-being. Experts from Kew's Millennium Seed Bank are working with the Forestry Commission on the UK National Tree Seed Project, collecting seeds of all the UK's native tree and shrub species. The collection will support conservation and research to help achieve national goals of increasing woodland cover across the UK. >>

MANAGING WOODLAND FOR WILDLIFE

The traditional management of Britain's woodlands creates valuable wildlife habitats. Historically they have also been put to many uses by people. The sessile oak, *Quercus petraea*, was used to build ships as well as houses, while the understorey shrubs were utilised for fencing, tool-making and fuel. Coppicing, a sustainable method of harvesting, was once common in Britain, and Kew has reintroduced the practice into the Natural Areas.

Hazel, *Corylus avellana*, sweet chestnut, *Castanea sativa*, and lime, *Tilia*, are left to grow as multi-stemmed shrubs for a few years and then their wood is harvested by cutting right back to their bases. All three species regenerate quickly, producing long straight stems that can be harvested again within a few years. The wood is used in the Gardens for plant supports and fencing and also to produce barbecue charcoal, which is sold through Kew retail outlets. Coppicing is carried out on a cyclical basis, bringing light into the glades, encouraging flowers like snowdrops, wild garlic and bluebells.

Rides, glades, coppice and wetlands encourage diversity in the Natural Areas, which ring with the song of birds like blackcap, dunnock, garden warbler, nuthatch and long-tailed tit. The chatter of greenfinches, chaffinches and treecreepers add

to the soundscape, while sparrowhawks hunt silently through the canopy and kestrels hover over grassy margins, looking for voles. Foxes and weasels can occasionally be seen, as can smaller mammals such as wood mouse and common shrew.

While decaying ancient trees, standing dead wood and falling timber have in former times been seen as symbols of neglect, they are now recognised as one of the Natural Areas' most important habitats. Up to a third of the woodland invertebrates depend on dead wood at some stage in their lifecycle, in turn supporting creatures further up the food chain like the great spotted woodpecker, which can be heard hammering at standing dead wood in its search for food. The high volume of dead wood in the area has also encouraged a rich fungal diversity that is not so evident in the rest of the Gardens. Kew's Stag Beetle Loggery A3 provides a safe haven for a globally endangered creature that depends on dead wood. The stag beetle is often seen at Kew in May and June. Its fearsome-looking antlers are actually jaws, but it is harmless, helping to return minerals from dead plants back to the soil. The larvae mature for up to seven years in rotting wood before turning into beetles.

Wetland is a further element in this wildlife tapestry. In the wildlife pond waterboatman, mayfly and damselfly are joined by amphibians – the common frog, common toad and the common or smooth newt. Visitors can watch the wildlife and learn more about it on the Woodland Walk trail. C1

Long-grass areas bring a naturalistic beauty here and across the Arboretum. Careful management is required to maintain a balance of plant species. Grasslands and meadows are valuable for invertebrates and these features are managed to maximise biodiversity. Grasshoppers and crickets lay eggs at the base of the grassland sward in late summer, so grass-cutting takes place as late in the year as possible and the clippings are removed. Kew ecologists are also helping to conserve acid grassland, an endangered native habitat which is important not only for rare plant species but also for the wide range of insects, reptiles and birds it supports. The scientists are experimenting with different seed mixes to see how they support the development of the habitat, which is particularly associated with that iconic songbird, the skylark.

Kew's arboriculturists help to make valuable new habitats out of old dead trees in the Natural Areas.

ART

Since the cave paintings of prehistoric times people have used art to represent nature, but over the last 400 years the science of botany has pushed the artist to new aesthetic and technical heights. Kew's world-leading collection of botanical art and illustration includes works by the great masters of the 18th century through to the celebrated artists who collaborate with our scientists today.

Throughout the Gardens, sculptures and statues are incorporated into the landscape and changing exhibitions seek to explore and enhance our profound connections with nature. Our rich collections of art, archives and artefacts show how people have made those connections with the wider world, through exploration, observation and craft.

Simon Verelst (1644– c.1721), Tulips, from the Kew Collection.

ART AND ARTEFACTS AT KEW

Kew is home to one of the world's greatest collections of botanical illustration, as well as a fine collection of portraits of people associated with botany and horticulture and over 250 objets d'art, ranging from sculptures to scientific instruments.

Alongside such art, the craft skills of cultures around the world are captured in Kew's Economic Botany Collection, which holds around 100,000 items, showing how humans use plants, through present-day material, archaeological specimens and 19th-century curiosities.

Often very beautiful in their own right are the letters, sketchbooks and field notes of botanists, gardeners and travellers held in Kew's archive. This rich historical resource – over 7 million sheets of paper – charts the discovery, study, transfer and use of the world's plants and fungi.

Kew's archives include extraordinary jewels such as a contemporary transcript of the journals written by Sir Joseph Banks as he travelled with Captain James Cook to the South Seas from 1768 to 1771. Sir Joseph Hooker's botanical drawings from his travels in the Antarctic and India are joined by his letters and notebooks, embellished with sketches of plants and landscape.

Also behind the scenes is Kew Library's collection of illustrated books, which includes fine volumes from the private library of Kew's first official director Sir William Hooker, such as Besler's *Hortus Eystettensis* of 1613, and other highly illustrated books including rarities like Jacquin's *Selectarum stirpium Americanarum historia* and John Sibthorp's

handcoloured ten-volume *Flora Graeca,* produced between 1806 and 1840, as well as many beautiful recently published items.

So how do our visitors explore these treasures? Our collections of botanical art and artefacts are regularly drawn upon for the annual cycle of exhibitions in our latest art space, the Shirley Sherwood Gallery of Botanical Art, while the unique Marianne North Gallery encompasses Victorian history at its most decorative and eccentric.

Statues and sculpture can be found throughout the Gardens, bringing another dimension to the changing landscape. The permanent collection is joined by many installations and works on loan for specific festivals, such as recent exhibitions of world-famous artists including Henry Moore, Dale Chihuly and David Nash.

You can book an appointment with Kew's archives team to view the original archive items in the public reading room. Items from the Library, one of the most important botanical references sources in the world, are also made available in the reading room. You can learn more about Kew's collections through Kew's website (www. kew.org), where you can also find a wonderful series of blogs revealing further stories from behind the scenes.

'A Sower' by Sir Hamo Thornycroft watches over the Grass Garden.

PURE QUININE.
5 grains one dose,
Price 1 pice.

Ginkgo biloba

The Economic Botany Collection at Kew illustrates the extent of human use of plants around the world, from food, medicine and utensils, to social activities and clothing. The collection forms an important bridge between biological and cultural diversity, valuable for the study of plant uses past, present and future.

TREASURES OF BOTANICAL ART

The Shirley Sherwood Gallery of Botanical Art is the first gallery in the world dedicated solely to botanical art. Open all year round, this elegant space exhibits works of art from Kew's extensive collection as well as from Dr Sherwood's own contemporary collection.

The focus of the Gallery G10 is botanical illustration – a fusion of science and art as vibrant and necessary today as it was in the early days of botany, before the advent of photography and the arrival of the digital age. The primary purpose of botanical art is to show scientific detail. It can reveal more than a photograph, depicting every stage of a plant's lifecycle from flower to seed, deliberately highlighting elements that cannot be distinguished with a camera. Yet the skilled artist also produces compositions of beauty and historical significance, taking their value far beyond technical accuracy.

Kew's world-leading collection includes works by the great masters of botanical illustration of the 18th century, such as Redouté and Kew's first official painter, Francis Bauer, who was engaged by Sir Joseph Banks in 1790. Many of the early originals were prepared for *Curtis's Botanical Magazine*, which dates back to 1789, and these are joined by the work of 19th- and 20th-century-contributors such as Walter Hood Fitch and Stella Ross-Craig and present-day artists such as Christabel King. There are special collections of specific artists, for example Margaret Mee (see right) and G D Ehret, who painted flowers for the Earl of Bute when he was advisor to Kew's founder Princess Augusta in the 1750s. Among them are also illustrations of extinct species for which the artwork may be the only surviving record.

Dr Shirley Sherwood has built one of the world's most comprehensive collections of contemporary botanical art. In 1990 she purchased an orchid painted by Kew artist Pandora Sellars and her

The Shirley Sherwood Gallery
of Botanical Art and the
Marianne North Gallery.

Pioneering conservationist
Margaret Mee (1909–1988) was
an outstanding botanical artist.
Her expeditions to the Brazilian
rainforest from 1956 to 1988
coincided with the period
of maximum deforestation
and Mee was one of the first
to raise a voice against the
destructive exploitation of
the Amazon. Kew holds 60 of
her original watercolour and
gouache paintings.

collection now represents work from over 300 artists
working in more than 35 countries, acquired during
her worldwide travels.

The Shirley Sherwood Gallery of Botanical Art
is next to the Marianne North Gallery and the two
buildings are joined together by the Link Gallery,
which displays contemporary botanical works from
the Sherwood Collection on a regularly changing
basis. The main gallery space stages two new
exhibitions each year, often drawing on Kew's art,
artefacts and treasures from the Library and Archives.
Works from partner institutions and the Sherwood
Collection also feature, with one exhibition each
year based extensively on the latter.

MARIANNE NORTH GALLERY

The Marianne North Gallery was purpose built in 1882 to house an exuberant display of botanical and landscape paintings by an intrepid and unconventional Victorian traveller.

Marianne North was 40 when she embarked on her first solo expedition in 1871, determined to 'paint the peculiar vegetation' of other lands. Over the next 13 years she travelled widely to destinations including North and South America, Japan, India, Australia and South Africa, capturing over 900 species in her own distinctive style. With minimal formal training, she worked using a palette of bold assertive colours, sketching rapidly in pen and ink on heavy paper, and painting with oils straight from the tube. In contrast to the scientific accuracy of botanical illustration, Marianne showed her subjects in their natural settings, sometimes with an associated insect, bird or other small creature. Her vast collection of 832 paintings thereby constitutes a snapshot in time of tropical and temperate habitats from across the globe.

In 1879, Marianne wrote to Sir Joseph Hooker offering Kew her collection and a gallery to house it. Her architect friend James Fergusson designed the Gallery which, with its veranda, echoes her attachment to India, while satisfying his own ideas on lighting with large clerestory windows high above the paintings.

Marianne took charge of the hanging, arranging her pictures in geographical sequence over a dado of 246 strips of different timbers. An extensive two-year project has now restored the Marianne North Gallery and its paintings to their original splendour and a linking gallery joins the Grade II listed building to the Shirley Sherwood Gallery of Botanical Art. Touch screen monitors in the Gallery allow visitors to zoom in on 50 of the paintings and read extracts from Marianne's memoirs. In the artist's studio, visitors can learn more about the artist and view a set of 'then and now' photos, which show how the landscapes in four paintings – in Jamaica, Sri Lanka, South Africa and Tasmania – have dramatically changed in the intervening years.

Many of Marianne North's paintings show her subjects in their natural habitats. You can learn more about Marianne in the Kew book *Marianne North, a very intrepid painter* and the DVD *The Remarkable Miss North* on sale in Kew's shops.

Apart from this monument to an extraordinary personality – and to the world view that prevailed in Victorian Britain – Kew's collections are enriched by associated material from Marianne North. Within the photographic collection there are several original photos of her taken by the famous photographer Julia Margaret Cameron (1815–1879), while Kew's archive holds letters from Marianne to various friends and acquaintances about both her travel experiences and the creation of the North Gallery at Kew Gardens, some including sketches.

Above: The 832 paintings are arranged geographically filling every inch of space in the purpose-built Victorian gallery. They were hung by Marianne North herself (right).

ARCHITECTURE

Kew Gardens began as two great royal estates and went on to become an economic powerhouse of empire. Now one of the world's leading centres for plant and fungi research, it is also a heritage site of global importance.

Its buildings come from every stage of its history, some ornamental, others designed to provide its valuable collections with the environments they need. In every case, the architects have employed the latest ideas and technology to ensure that their buildings are both fit for purpose and beautiful to behold.

You can see a range of architectural gems at Kew from 17th century palaces to Victorian glasshouses, and now cutting-edge design too. The Hive was the award-winning UK Pavilion at the World Expo in Milan in 2015. It came to Kew in 2016 and reveals the world of the honeybee and our changing relationship with these vital pollinators.

BUILDINGS AT KEW

Kew has 38 listed buildings including glasshouses, gateways and follies. Alongside these sit the contemporary designs of the modern era. The development of architectural design over time is reflected in these buildings.

Building plans not to scale.

Kew Palace

1631. Built for the rich Flemish merchant Samuel Fortrey, this palace became a country retreat for George III and his family.

Great Pagoda

1762. A fashionable Chinoiserie folly designed by Sir Willam Chambers to grace the pleasure gardens of Princess Augusta.

Palm House

1848. The Palm House used the latest innovations in ship-building and glazing to create a palace for rainforest plants.

Waterlily House

1852. Once the widest single-span glasshouse in the world, built to house tropical waterlilies and climbing plants.

Temperate House

1862–1899. The Temperate House was built over several decades to house frost-tender plants. An ambitious five-year restoration was completed in 2018.

Princess of Wales Conservatory

1987. Ten landscaped zones house plants from cool deserts to tropical mountains, cloud forests and rainforests.

Davies Alpine House

2006. This ingenious alpine house is designed like a cooling tower for plants from the world's mountain regions.

Shirley Sherwood Gallery of Botanical Art and Marianne North Gallery

2008 and 1882. These two purpose-built galleries hold magnificent collections of botanical illustration and art.

ROYAL TREASURES

The first century of Kew Gardens was intimately bound up with the Royal Family. This peaceful, leafy estate along the River Thames was a retreat from the demands of court and the filth and chaos of London.

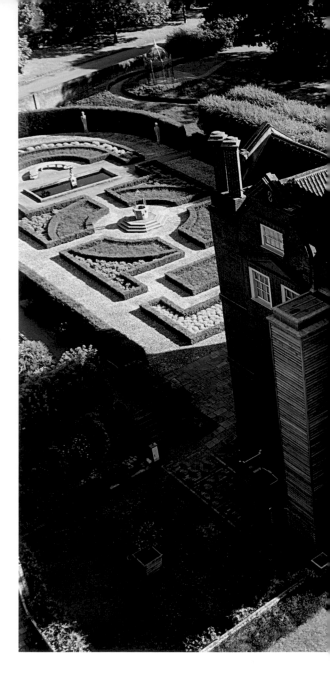

George II and his descendants built palaces, follies and temples to adorn the landscape and to provide accommodation fit for kings. But while Kew Palace (right) O 3 is the oldest building in the Gardens and the last surviving royal residence, its modest interiors encapsulate Georgian taste and style, rather than palatial opulence. Built in 1631 for a rich Flemish merchant called Samuel Fortrey, it was originally known as the Dutch House and the first royal residents were the three elder daughters of George II.

Their brother Frederick, Prince of Wales, lived opposite them in a large Palladian palace called the White House – since demolished – and it was here that his son, the future King George III, grew up. At Kew Palace he received the extensive education that was to profoundly influence his reign, a period in which ideas of science, art and manufacturing blossomed. Even when he became King, George disliked court life, retreating to his country estates to explore the latest ideas in agriculture and architecture. He and his wife, Queen Charlotte, spent happy summers at Kew Palace with their 15 children and it was an important refuge during his infamous episodes of 'madness'. After Queen Charlotte died in 1818, Kew Palace was shut up. It was acquired by Kew in 1898 and opened to the public for the first time. Today it is in the trust of Historic Royal Palaces.

Close to Kew Palace, the Georgian Royal Kitchens remain miraculously preserved, 200 years after they were last used. Designed by one of the greatest architects of his day, William Kent, their dimensions give us an idea of the grand scale of the White House. The great kitchen is an impressive double-height room, complete with roasting range, charcoal grill and pastry oven, while in four adjacent rooms bread was baked, fish and meat stored, vegetables prepared and pots and pans scoured with sand and soap in the lead-lined sink. Upstairs is the office of the clerk, who was responsible for feeding the enormous royal household. He held under lock and key the expensive spices, sugar, cinnamon and other luxuries.

The botanic garden founded by George III's mother, Princess Augusta, would be instrumental in bringing many of these precious commodities to the tables of an emerging middle-class.

CLASSICAL PROPORTION

The Orangery (right) P4 is a fine classical building constructed in 1761 and designed by Sir William Chambers to house citrus trees and other ornamentals. However, even with the addition of two side windows in 1842 the light levels were never high enough for plants to thrive inside. Chambers created many of the ornamental buildings that still provide focal points in the Gardens today including the Great Pagoda.

AUDACIOUS FOLLY

The Great Pagoda C 9 was completed in 1762 as a gift for Princess Augusta, the founder of the botanic gardens at Kew. It was one of several Chinese buildings here, including a bridge and an aviary, designed by royal architect Sir William Chambers at a time when Chinoiserie was the height of fashion. The Pagoda was originally flanked by a Moorish Alhambra and a Turkish Mosque – follies that helped bring the architecture of the world to Kew. As symbols of fashion, wealth and power, these garden ornaments were the subject of much public comment. The Pagoda was judged 'a whimsical object', 'the puerile effort of an overgrown boy' and 'a masterpiece of art' as revealed in Ray Desmond's authoritative *History of the Royal Botanic Gardens, Kew*.

During the construction of the Pagoda, the politician Horace Walpole, who lived in nearby Twickenham, wrote 'We begin to perceive the tower of Kew from Montpelier Row; in a fortnight you will be able to see it in Yorkshire.' The ten-storey octagonal structure is nearly 50m high (163 ft) and the uppermost level is reached by a staircase of 253 steps. Contemporary commentators wondered that such a tall building could remain standing but its tapering design gives it great stability, each successive floor being 30 cm (1 ft) less in both diameter and height than the one below it.

Throughout the 20th century the Great Pagoda was painted a bright postbox-red, but Chambers' original colour scheme was much more colourful. Historic Royal Palaces has restored this glorious folly and their detailed paint analysis has shown that the window frames and balustrades were once a warm stony white, while the window casements and the top roof were Venetian red. The undersides of the ten roofs were striped in green and white, which change in ratio to give the building an impression of being taller than it is. A return to Chambers' 18th-century scheme brings historic integrity back to this spectacular building, but, best of all, it has also brought back the dragons. The Pagoda was designed and built with 80 crouching dragons perching on the hips of the roofs, but little was known about them as they disappeared in 1784. After much research, they have now been recreated and painted in their original bright colours of 'copper verdigris', red, blue and gold, adding wonderful drama to this corner of the Gardens.

You can visit the Pagoda and take in the stunning views from the top while learning more about Kew and the Georgians. Nearby you'll find a new Chinese landscape full of beautiful plants of Chinese origin and the stories of how they came to our gardens.

Kew's handsome classical Nash Conservatory is the oldest of Kew's 19th century glasshouses. Originally one of four pavilions designed by John Nash for the gardens at Buckingham Palace, it was moved to Kew by King William IV in 1836.

PALACES OF GLASS

One of the most important Victorian structures still in existence, the Palm House has stood at the heart of Kew Gardens for 170 years.

Shortly after the Gardens passed from the Crown to the nation the Palm House K 7 was built to meet the urgent need to house the palms and other tropical trees that were being dispatched to Kew from around the world. It was the hub of Nesfield's landscape design, which unified the historically distinct estates, with vistas radiating from its west doors to the far reaches of the site.

THE PALM HOUSE

The Palm House was built using the latest technological innovations. It was constructed between 1844 and 1848 by engineer Richard Turner to Decimus Burton's design. The elegant curvilinear structure, with its large central hall unimpeded by pillars, was only made possible by recent developments in shipbuilding and glazing. It was heated by a system of pipes fed by 12 boilers, circulating warm air through an iron grating floor. An underground tunnel was used to deliver fuel to the furnaces and carried the smoke away to a chimney, disguised as an Italian Romanesque campanile, which can still be seen towering over Victoria Gate.

The Palm House measures 110 m (363 ft) long, 30 m (100 ft) wide and 19 m (63 ft) high. In spite of the fact that it was originally clad in 16,000 panes of green-tinted glass, it eventually proved to be a

The Palm House combined Victorian technology and Imperial ambition to create a home for some of the world's most important tropical plants.

Kew's Waterlily House opened in 1852. At the time it was the widest single-span glasshouse in the world, purpose-built to house the natural wonder of the age, the giant waterlily, *Victoria amazonica*. Today, you can see its close relative *Victoria cruziana* here, while *V. amazonica* is grown in the Princess of Wales Conservatory. Both put on glorious displays every summer, alongside *Nymphaea* waterlilies and sacred lotus, *Nelumbo nucifera*.

horticultural success. The first palms, cycads and trees in the Palm House were planted in large teak tubs or clay pots and within five years Turner's elegant spiral staircases and wrought iron balustrades were smothered by climbers. In 1860, two large central beds were dug and the tallest palms planted in them. Freed from their pots the trees thrived, several species flowering for the first time outside the tropics, and gradually most of the plants were transferred to beds.

The Palm House was first restored between 1955 and 1957 when its glazing bars were cleaned and the entire house re-glazed. A second more comprehensive overhaul took place between 1984 and 1988. The Grade I listed-building was emptied, completely dismantled, restored and rebuilt. Ten miles of replica glazing bars made of stainless steel were put in place to hold new panes of toughened safety glass. The restoration took as long to finish as the glasshouse first took to build.

THE TEMPERATE HOUSE

Once the largest glasshouse in the world and now the world's largest surviving Victorian glass structure, the Temperate House has recently undergone an ambitious five-year architectural restoration. Now back to its original gleaming splendour, the Temperate House re-opened in 2018.

Another spectacular Decimus Burton design, the Temperate House is twice the size of the Palm House at 4,880 square metres. It was built over several decades (1862–1899) to house frost-tender plants from the sub-tropical and warm temperate regions of the world. Burton designed the planting beds so that species could be displayed by geographical region and this is still the case today, although many more regions are now represented than in the 19th century.

In the central section of the house you'll find plants from Central and South America, New Zealand, Australia and from islands around the world including those on which Kew has active conservation programmes including St Helena. The north wing, nearest King William's Temple, holds plants from Asia, while in the south wing, nearest the Great Pagoda, you'll discover the flora of South Africa. In total the Temperate House is now home to over 10,000 plants of 1,500 species – an extremely important scientific collection that is both vital for conservation and beautiful to visit.

The restoration of this complex and ornate glasshouse has been done to exacting heritage standards and included repairing much of the elaborate stonework, urns, statuary, window frames and ironwork. Extensive new leading had to be completed and 15,000 panes of glass were replaced. New walkways throughout the house now afford visitors better views of the plants and the stunning new water features. The octagons are now places to enjoy changing educational and horticultural displays.

Take time to explore the newly opened house and delight in the restored architecture and the many special and useful plants on display here. Make sure you talk to the explainers, who are on hand to share intriguing plant stories and can point out the highlights of the collections to you, including the Wood's cycad, *Encephalartos woodii*, St Helena olive, *Nesiota elliptica*, marsh heath, *Erica verticillata*, *Banksia brownii* and *Dombeya mauritiana* to name but a few.

Take a tour of the newly restored Temperate House to discover stories of rare and threatened plants, and Kew's work in the temperate regions of the world to study and conserve plant diversity for the benefit of everyone.

CONTEMPORARY ICONS

The architects of Kew's extraordinary 19th-century glasshouses created structures that were not only beautiful but purpose-built for the greatest plant collection in the world. Two award-winning glasshouses at the north end of the Gardens extend this fine tradition into the modern age.

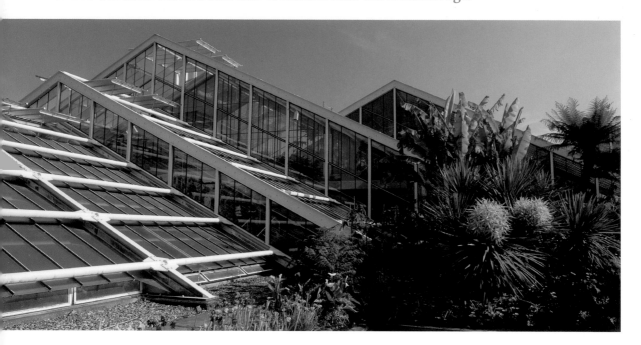

PRINCESS OF WALES CONSERVATORY

The Princess of Wales Conservatory (above) N 7 was opened in 1987 by Diana, Princess of Wales, and is named after her predecessor Princess Augusta, the founder of the botanic gardens at Kew. Its dramatic angled gables and its surrounding landscaped beds are a sleek rejoinder to the curves of the Palm House and the classical ornament of the Temperate House. Designed by Gordon Wilson to achieve the highest possible energy efficiency, its stepped glass roof is an extremely effective collector of solar energy and much of the building lies below ground level, which insulates it against heat loss. Inside, paths, steps, bridges and tunnels lead the visitor through ten landscaped zones, their temperature and humidity carefully controlled to recreate a range of environments, from tropical desert to rainforest (see p16).

DAVIES ALPINE HOUSE

The most recent glasshouse built at Kew is also the smallest. The glass and steel arch of the Davies Alpine House (right) O 8 rises lightly over the northern sandstone terraces of the Rock Garden. It is designed to keep plants dry in winter (when they would naturally lie under a blanket of snow) and provide the cool summer conditions of their mountain habitats, without using energy-intensive air-conditioning and wind pumps. To counteract the build up of heat that always occurs under glass, the distinctive structure acts like a chimney; as warm air escapes through vents in the roof, cool air is drawn in at the base. Meanwhile, a fan blows air through a concrete labyrinth beneath the ground. The air cools on its convoluted journey and flows over the plants from a series of funnels within the rocky landscape. The laminated glass has an extremely low iron content, allowing 90% of daylight through. Alpines from high altitudes thrive in the resulting intense sunlight. However, in extremely hot periods the temperature in the house is regulated by shading provided by four beautiful fan-shaped sails. Designed by Wilkinson-Eyre Associates, the Davies Alpine House was awarded a prestigious RIBA award for architecture when it opened in 2006.

TREETOP WALKWAY

While Kew's glasshouses and galleries focus on their contents, another striking contemporary structure offers thrilling perspectives on the great outdoors. At 18 m (59 ft) above the ground, Kew's Treetop Walkway G6 gives visitors a rare insight into the complex ecosystem of the forest canopy, a world teeming with birds and insects, lichens and fungi. The 200 m (656 ft) long walkway was opened in 2008, designed by Marks Barfield Architects, who also designed the London Eye, and won numerous awards in 2009 including the RIBA Award, the Structural Steel Design Award and the Civic Trust Award.

Made from over 400 tonnes of weathered steel, the 12 walkway trusses connect ten 'node' platforms, including one large enough to provide a lofty, open air classroom for school groups. Far-reaching views across the Gardens and over the London skyline show the vital part trees play in the landscape, not only contributing to its beauty but providing habitats for urban wildlife and acting as natural air conditioners (just a 10% increase in urban greenery can cut the temperature in a city by up to four degrees centigrade in summer).

Above: High up on the Walkway, visitors experience the scale and seasonal cycle of beech, lime, oak, sweet and horse chestnut trees.

SACKLER CROSSING

Opened in 2006 the Sackler Crossing is the first ever bridge across the Lake, designed by the architect John Pawson. Winner of the 2008 Stephen Lawrence Prize, the striking black granite walkway guides visitors low over the water along a curving path that mimics the Lake's rounded banks. Its walls are a series of vertical, flat bronze posts. On approaching the Crossing these give the appearance of forming a solid wall, but when viewed sideways on they appear almost invisible. This is akin to the ways in which water can appear both solid and fluid.

The design of the trusses of the Treetop Walkway is inspired by the Fibonacci sequence, a number series found frequently in natural growth patterns. You can see this pattern in the complex spirals of the sunflower.

SHIRLEY SHERWOOD GALLERY OF BOTANICAL ART

The Shirley Sherwood Gallery of Botanical Art G10 is the first public gallery dedicated to botanical art, displaying treasures from Kew's collections (see p66) alongside works from the collection of Dr Shirley Sherwood and partner institutions. Award-winning architects Walters and Cohen employed the latest technologies to provide controlled conditions to keep the artworks in perfect condition, but with minimal environmental impact. In 2018, the Gallery celebrated its tenth anniversary.

The glazed exterior of the beautifully proportioned pavilion provides an elegant counterbalance to the Victorian ornament of the adjacent Marianne North Gallery (see p68–69).

THE HIVE

The Hive O 5 is a unique and critically acclaimed structure, inspired by scientific research into the health of bees. Designed by UK-based artist Wolfgang Buttress, it was originally created as the centrepiece of the UK Pavilion at the 2015 World Expo in Milan, which had the theme of 'Feeding the Planet, Energy for Life'.

The Hive is an open-air structure standing at 17 m (56 ft) tall and weighing in at 40 tonnes. It is made from around 170,000 individual components that together create an intriguing lattice or honeycomb-like effect. Inside you'll find around 900 LED lights that glow and fade as a unique soundscape hums and buzzes around you. The Hive encapsulates the story of honeybees and their important role in pollinating crops and other plants.

The multi-sensory elements of light and sound within the Hive are in fact responding to the real-time activity of bees in a beehive behind the scenes at Kew. Their intensity within the space changes as the energy levels in the real beehive surge, giving visitors an insight into life inside a bee colony.

The Hive has its own soundscape called *One*, which is a constantly changing piece of meditative music in the key of C that merges improvised music with the sound of 40,000 bees in a hive, creating a truly immersive audio experience.

Around the Hive you'll find a meadow with 34 native wildflower species including selfheal, ox-eye daisies and ragged robin, which flower over the summer and autumn. There are also 19 non-native species beneficial to bees including California poppies, soapwort, blue flax and hyssop. The space is edged with native hedgerow species including hawthorn, guelder rose and wayfaring tree, which also support bees and other wildlife.

Bees are fundamental to human existence because they pollinate a large number of the crops that feed us. During peak visitor seasons you'll find explainers near the Hive who will share fascinating information with you about the installation and about the life of honeybees, and can also point you towards the beehives in the Plant Family Beds O 8 .

LINE OF EXISTING GROUND LEVEL

CHANGING LANDSCAPE

The landscape of Kew Gardens is as significant as its plant collections and its architecture. The vistas and glades represent ideas about nature and science as they have developed over 250 years. Lakes and lawns frame Kew's iconic buildings and the great displays of trees and flowers paint complex ever-changing panoramas through which the visitor can explore this tranquil, historic place.

Kew's World Heritage Site landscape is a green oasis in busy west London, offering secluded gardens, expansive vistas and spectacular glasshouses.

LIVING HISTORY

Kew's complex history is imprinted upon its landscape. Its contours and plant collections chart three centuries of development, from royal pleasure ground to people's park, from pastoral idyll through the frenzied collection of exotics and the industrial exploitation of natural resources, to a national reference collection informing conservation, medical and genetic research.

Now encompassing 132 hectares (326 acres), the site is bound by the River Thames to the west, the beautiful eastern wall along Kew Road, the elegant Kew Green to the north, and Richmond's leafy deer park to the south. At every point, the visitor is beckoned by views, ornaments, buildings and extraordinary plants, each with a fascinating story. These multiple layers of history, science, culture and personality are celebrated in Kew's status as a UNESCO World Heritage Site.

TREND-SETTING ROYAL ESTATES

The Gardens were born of the ambitions of two powerful 18th-century women who sought to present the latest fashionable thinking through their adjacent royal estates. Queen Caroline pioneered the English Landscape Garden style – with no expense spared – while her daughter-in-law, Princess Augusta, embraced Enlightenment ideas of purpose and pleasure by founding a botanic garden at the heart of her Chinoiserie-style landscape.

Queen Caroline, wife of King George II, engaged Charles Bridgeman to redesign Richmond Gardens in the mid-1720s. Formal baroque terraces and avenues were swept away and this flat expanse of floodplain, with the River Thames at its western boundary, was sculpted and planted to create an Arcadian landscape of walks and woodland, interspersed by arable fields. William Kent's Hermitage, his famous gothic Merlin's Cave and other follies enhanced this recreation of rural idyll. Lancelot 'Capability' Brown, one of the most famous

landscapers in Britain's history, further developed the naturalistic character of Richmond Gardens in the first decades after George III ascended the throne. Kent's whimsical buildings and the beloved riverside terrace were replaced by sweeping lawns and artful clusters of trees. Brown's picturesque Hollow Walk of 1773 survives as the Rhododendron Dell. Another rustic element that can still be seen in the south-western

Dairy House

REFERENCES

1 Terrass opposite Richmond Green
2 Wallnut tree Walk
3 Chesnut Walk
4 Kings Palace
5 Wild Chesnut Walk
6 Glass House
7 Green House
8 Managery
9 Kitchen Green
10 Flower Border
11 Court Yard
12 Stables
13 Queens Walk
14 Old Deer Park
15 Great Elms Walk
16 Sybon Walk
17 Ice House
18 Dairy House

20 The Mount
21 Dry Pond
22 Tarrass
23 Summer House on Ditto
24 Oak Walks
25 Wilderness call'd Keepers Close
26 Keepers House
27 Ducks Pond
28 Pheasants House
29 Hermitage
30 Amphitheatre form'd by Elms
31 Brentford Ferry
32 Isleworth Ferry
33 The Princess of Wales's House at Kew
34 His Royal Highness & Prince of Wales's house at Kew
35 Great Terrass
36 Iron Gates

THE RIVER THAMES

the Right Honble the Duke of Northumberland

HERMITAGE

SION HOUSE

Pheasant Ground

Love Lane

XACT PLAN OF THE ROYAL
Gardens and Park at
RICHMOND
ON HOUSE &c. on the Opposite Side
ames. SURVEY'D & Publish'd by
hn Rocque Chorographer
to his
NESS'S THE PRINCE OF WALES

PLAN DU PALAIS
Jardins et Parc de Richmond
à 8 Miles de LONDRES
levé et Publié par Jean Rocque
Chorographe de S.A.R. Monseigneur
le PRINCE DE GALLES.

500   1000   1500

Echelle de 250 Toises

RENVOY

1 Terrasse vis à vis de Richmond Green
2 Allée de Noyers
3 Allée de Chataigniers
4 Maison Royale
5 Allée de Marronniers
6 Serre pour les Plantes Etrangeres
7 Serre pour les Orangers
8 La Menagerie
9 Jardin Potager
10 Platte Bande de Fleurs
11 La Basse Cour
12 Les Ecuries
13 Allée de la Reine
14 Le vieux Parc aux Cerfs
15 Allée de Grand Ormeaux
16 Allée de Tybon
17 La Glaciere
18 Laitterie
19 Le Canal

20 Le Moloquay
21 Etang See
22 La Terrasse
23 Salon de la Terrasse
24 Allée de Chêne
26 Maison du Garde
27 Etang des Cannards

28 La Phaisanderie
29 L'Hermitage
30 Amphitheatre formé par des Ormeaux
31 Bac de Brentford
32 Bac de Isleworth
33 Maison de la Princesse de Galles à Kew
34 Maison de Son Altesse Royale le Prince de Galles à Kew
35 La Grande Terrasse
36 Grilles de Fer
37 Grote de Merlin

corner of today's Gardens is Queen Charlotte's Cottage. An early example of a *cottage orné*, the thatched building was used by the Royal Family in the late 18th century for rest and refreshment during walks in the gardens. Exotic animals were kept in the paddock to the rear of the cottage, including colourful pheasants and the first kangaroos to arrive in England. >>

William Andrews Nesfield's design for the landscape at Kew centred around the Palm House and included the formal parterre on its east side.

FASHION RIVALS

Princess Augusta, wife of Prince Frederick and mother of the future George III, was to promote an even more flamboyant, exotic style in her garden at Kew. Statuary, formal shrub plantings, lawns and hedged fields of the 1730s were gradually embellished by 'curious & forain' trees, a lake and mount. However, it was after Frederick's unexpected death in 1751 that work began in earnest to implement his plan for the Kew garden. Guided by the Earl of Bute, mentor to the future George III, Princess Augusta founded the botanic garden, a five acre arboretum and a physic garden. Her burgeoning tree collection – in particular, new introductions from North America – was laid out according to the new method of bi-nomial classification devised by Swedish botanist Carl Linnaeus – each plant uniquely identified by two Latin words. Within ten years, the list of Kew's plants – *Hortus Kewensis* – listed 3,400 species.

FOLLIES IN THE PLEASURE GROUNDS

At the same time, the architect Sir William Chambers began to create buildings for the Princess's pleasure grounds, among them the Great Pagoda and the Orangery. Of his many follies – ornamental architectural features of little practical use – four remain, all of them Grade II listed buildings. The Temple of Arethusa (1758) K 8 is named after a nymph attendant of Diana, Roman goddess of hunting. Today this temple is the setting for Kew's war memorials and is adorned with wreaths every

11 November. The Ruined Arch (1759) F10 is a charming mock ruin in classical Roman style; the Temple of Bellona (1760) I 9 , with its Doric facade, is named after the Roman goddess of war and pays tribute to the British and Hanoverian regiments which fought in the Seven Years' War; the Temple of Aeolus (1760) M8 , named after the mythical king of storms and the four winds, was originally built of wood and once had a revolving seat to provide a panoramic view of the whole Kew estate. It was rebuilt in stone by Decimus Burton in 1845.

ORNAMENTAL LAWNS

As European explorers charted the world, both gardens were developed to display exciting newly-discovered plants. New technology affected not only the architecture but the landscape too. In the 18th century, Kew's pastures were grazed by livestock, but over the decades, the gradual mechanisation of grass cutting led to the long tradition of close-cropped ornamental lawns. Nineteenth-century garden design saw the lawn as the perfect foil for the major structural elements of the landscape – including the latest plant introductions from around the world, as well as terracing and parterres, reintroduced after being swept away in Georgian times.

In 1840, just as the idea of public parks had begun to take root, the Royal Botanic Gardens, Kew was transferred from the Crown to the nation. Under the directorship of Sir William Hooker, followed by his son Sir Joseph Hooker, it became a destination for public recreation and education. Its landscape was reconfigured as parkland and a fitting backdrop for monumental architecture, symbolising its new role as a driver of economic development across the British Empire.

VICTORIAN FORMALITY

William Andrews Nesfield, the leading exponent of renewed formality in gardens, unified the historically distinct estates by imposing on them a series of long vistas, which radiated out from the new Palm House, its pond and parterres. The Palm House complex was linked by the stately Broad Walk to a grand new entrance on Kew Green. Instead of an inconspicuous door in the boundary wall, visitors now entered the

Gardens through Decimus Burton's ornate gateway with Jacobean-style ironwork and carved stone pillars. This gate was renamed Elizabeth Gate in 2012 to mark HM Queen's Diamond Jubilee.

The construction of the Lake – now transformed by the beautiful Sackler Crossing G4 – and Waterlily Pond D4 added drama to the Arboretum. Popular demand for seasonal floral displays drove the development of hundreds of flower beds, incorporating the geometric style of the day, and the first Refreshment Pavilion, which opened in 1888.

Above: Temple of Aeolus, focus of the Woodland Garden.

Left: William Marlow's view of the Lake seen from the Great Lawn, with the Great Pagoda.

Pine Tree
Wilderness

Oak Tree Cir

Sun Garden

Water Garden

THE CHILDREN'S GARDEN

The new Children's Garden M4 will fascinate, excite and inspire children, with a combination of beautiful planting and outdoor play. Set amongst over 100 mature trees, the one hectare site near Brentford Gate has been designed to appeal to children under 12 years old and is themed around what plants need to grow: earth, air, sun and water.

In the Earth Garden is a vast sand pit, with wooden boardwalks and play huts to hide in. Children can clamber up a 3 metre high mound to descend down tubular 'worm hole' slides. The Air Garden includes trampolines, hammocks and a forest of 'wind flowers' that spin in the breeze. The Sun Garden is a wide open space surrounded by flowering cherry trees and a tunnel of hoops, on which fruit trees will grow. In the Water Garden, children can pump water down rocky channels and divert the flow with sluice gates before it reaches a shallow pool.

The Pine Tree Wilderness is an area for more adventurous play, with challenging climbs, a log bridge and a 5 metre tall leaning tower. The centre point of the whole garden is an elevated walkway, the Oak Tree Circle, that gives views of the garden and takes children up to the canopy of an old oak tree.

arth Garden

Air Garden

SCIENTIFIC PURPOSE OF THE GARDENS

In spite of the new emphasis on spectacle and public recreation, the scientific purpose of the Gardens remained at its core. A series of straight beds were laid out with plants grouped according to the latest scientific system of classification. Trees and shrubs were planted taxonomically in the Arboretum, and the Pinetum extended. One of the best holly, *Ilex*, collections in Europe still remains along Holly Walk H6 , while old excavations were exploited to create intimate oases like the Bamboo Garden H3 and Berberis Dell I9 .

The Hollow Walk became the Rhododendron Dell I2 , planted with Joseph Hooker's celebrated collections from Sikkim. The Rock Garden N8 and the first Alpine House were constructed and the Temperate House completed. By 1902, 8,000 herbaceous plants and 4,500 hardy trees and shrubs were recorded in cultivation.

There have been significant additions since the turn of the 20th century, such as the Grass Garden (see p41), the Rose Garden K7 to the west of the Palm House and the Japanese Gateway (see p38). Cherry Walk was created and, in 1911, the Rhododendron Dell was enhanced by the Chinese rhododendrons introduced by E H Wilson, and new buildings such as the Princess of Wales Conservatory (see p82) and the Treetop Walkway (see p84) have been added. However, by the end of Queen Victoria's reign, the Gardens had become essentially the landscape we see today.

Right: The Children's Garden

THE ROLE OF KEW

The Royal Botanic Gardens, Kew is a plant wonderland, maintained to inspire, inform and amaze our visitors. And with our Herbarium, Fungarium, DNA bank and Millennium Seed Bank it forms the most comprehensive plant reference collection on Earth, underpinning our science and conservation work with an international network of partners.

Kew has always brought excitement and intense curiosity to the scientific investigation of the natural world. We are a global resource for plant and fungal knowledge. At a time of dramatic environmental change, we are using that knowledge to address great challenges: feeding, healing and sheltering a growing population while conserving priceless natural resources.

COLLECTING AND ANALYSING

Kew's development was driven first by a hunger for exotic plants and then by the economic needs of an expanding empire, but the same drivers created the wealth of scientific knowledge and the extraordinary collections which underpin our work today.

Taxonomists at Kew are still discovering hundreds of new species of plants and fungi each year. But why is this knowledge important? And what impact can Kew's work make on the world? Botanists estimate that up to 100,000 species of flowering plants remain undiscovered while for fungi, the number is orders of magnitude greater. Nevertheless, every year the discovery of new species completes sections of the jigsaw.

Discovering and documenting plants and fungi help us to answer urgent questions; how and why evolution has taken certain paths; which species and habitats are at risk of extinction and how we can conserve them; what role plants and fungi play in ecosystems and how they can be used sustainably; and how global environmental change will affect plants, fungi and, ultimately, all life on Earth.

Kew's Herbarium is one of the largest in the world, housing more than 7 million dried, preserved plant specimens.

WORKING TO COMPLETE THE PICTURE

Deciding whether something is a new species is a complex task. Our living collections are complemented by an even greater collection of preserved plants and fungi, against which discoveries in the wild can be compared. Our Fungarium is the largest in the world and our Herbarium holds over seven million dried plant specimens, including collections made by some of Britain's most celebrated scientists and explorers, such as Joseph Banks, Charles Darwin, Joseph Hooker and David Livingstone. Today, hundreds of researchers come to Kew each year to study this resource and, in an ongoing programme of digitisation, images of half a million specimens can now be accessed on the web from anywhere in the world. Through our international networks, the jigsaw pieces are slotting together.

In 2015, Kew published the 2020 Science Strategy outlining its key objectives for future research, conservation and education endeavours. One objective was to publish a ground-breaking State of the World's Plants report each year – an easy to access 'health check' on the plant and fungal kingdoms, helping to focus research where it is most needed. You can view these future reports on www.kew.org, where you can also read blog posts from a range of Kew's scientists.

DNA AND THE PLANT FAMILY TREE

Over the past two decades, we have made great leaps in understanding how and when plants and fungi have evolved. Using DNA analysis, scientists in the Jodrell Laboratory, working as part of the Angiosperm Phylogeny Group (APG), have revised the family tree of all flowering plants, reclassifying them according to their genetic similarities. In 2016, the latest version of this new taxonomic system, known as APG IV, was published, and is a tool of global significance. Now, by looking at the complex web of relationships between plants, fungi and other organisms, we can find answers about what drives this evolution. A large team of Kew scientists work in our Jodrell Laboratory, harnessing new analytical techniques to pursue this understanding.

INFLUENCING INTERNATIONAL POLICY

Global environmental change is one of the greatest concerns of the 21st century, yet its impact on biodiversity, ecosystems and livelihoods remains uncertain.

With our vast store of historical and contemporary data, Kew is well-placed to predict the consequences of global change and to connect our science with policy and delivery on the ground. As the UK Scientific Authority for Plants, we work with and support the UK Government so it can meet its commitments under the Convention on International Trade in Endangered Species (CITES) and the European Union Wildlife Trade Regulations. And we develop analytical tools to aid the enforcement of these agreements and regulations. For example, using our living, preserved and ethnobotanical collections, we have developed DNA barcoding for plants – genetic markers – so that traded plants can be rapidly identified by customs officers and forensic scientists.

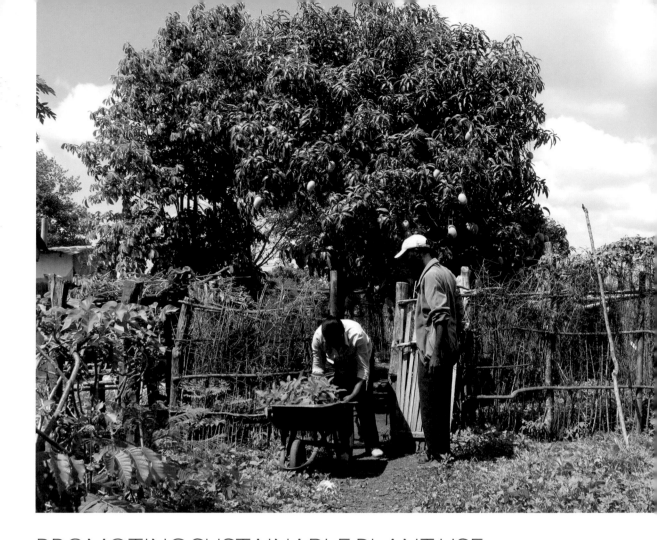

PROMOTING SUSTAINABLE PLANT USE

Healthy habitats support human livelihoods. We are experts in the many different ways that plants and fungi are used by people and we apply science to help communities develop sustainable practices.

Kew carries out research on useful plants from across the wild to domesticated spectrum. In Africa and Latin America, Kew is working with local communities to study, conserve and sustainably use indigenous plants which are adapted to the local conditions and important for their livelihoods. This is achieved through their conservation in seedbanks, propagation and planting in the communities, and the promotion of sustainable economic activities. In Colombia, Kew is working in partnership with various local organisations to support the sustainable development of Colombia's biodiversity resources through a robust scientific programme.

FINDING NEW MEDICINES

Among many research strands at Kew, we are working to identify plants with medicinal or economic potential. For example, plants from the Gardens and the Herbarium have been used to study chemical compounds from different species of *Plectranthus* – a member of the mint family – to find out the extent of their anti-malarial and insect-repellant properties, as well as their activity against bacteria, especially tuberculosis. Likewise, studying the chemistry of fungi is expected to reveal medical and agricultural applications as well as uses in food, drink and cosmetics.

BANKING SEED

We know that a fifth of the world's plants are at risk of extinction. Losing species can disrupt or damage ecosystems, which in turn can have severe consequences for people.

Kew's Millennium Seed Bank Partnership is the only global network dedicated to conserving wild plant seeds. Focusing on endangered species and plants of most use for the future, we conserve seeds as an insurance against the risk of extinction in their native habitat. Working with our partners across 96 countries, we have successfully banked over 13% of the world's wild plant species – including 78% of the threatened UK flora – both in their countries of origin and in our cutting-edge storage facility, the Millennium Seed Bank. We continue to pioneer seed storage and germination technology and by 2020 we will have banked 75,000 species.

Banking seed is only part of the complex process of conserving species. Reintroduction of native species to restore ecosystems is an even greater challenge. Kew collaborates on local and international levels to make this happen. Kew, in partnership with the Turks and Caicos Islands Government, has developed a restoration strategy to secure the National Tree of the Turks and Caicos Islands, the Caicos pine (*Pinus caribaea* var. *bahamensis*). Trees are being propagated locally and seeds collected for *ex situ* conservation in an effort to save the species and restore the local pine forests from the devastation caused by the non-native invasive pine tortoise scale insect.

By working closely with local botanists in Mexico and the Dominican Republic, we are exploring the most biodiverse forests to collect and bank seed from useful or threatened tree species. These seeds are then available for scientific research and the information produced is useful for forestry and community organisations. We continue to work with Addis Ababa University and the Ethiopian Biodiversity Institute to document and collect high profile endemic plant species of Ethiopia, amassing valuable information to help conserve them.

VISIT WAKEHURST

The Millennium Seed Bank can be visited at Kew's wild botanic garden at Wakehurst in West Sussex. Set in the dramatic landscape of the High Weald, Wakehurst's 188 hectares (465 acres) include ornamental and water gardens, temperate woodlands, the Loder Valley Nature Reserve and an Elizabethan mansion. Many important plant collections thrive in the higher rainfall and moister soils – especially from eastern Asia, South America, Australia and New Zealand. Find out more at www.kew.org/wakehurst

Around 2 billion seeds
are stored at −20 degrees
centigrade in the vault of the
Millennium Seed Bank, where
they can be accessed for
research and restoration work.

FURTHER READING

Brereton, Catherine and McGuiness, Jane. (2018). *Kew Children's Guide*. Bloomsbury in association with Kew.

Bynum, Helen and William. (2014). *Remarkable Plants That Shape Our World*. Thames & Hudson in association with Kew.

Clennett, Chris and Price, Katherine. (2015). *Wakehurst Guide*. Royal Botanic Gardens, Kew.

Cope, Tom. (2009). *The Wild Flora of Kew Gardens: A cumulative checklist from 1759*. Royal Botanic Gardens, Kew.

Desmond, Ray. (2007). *The History of the Royal Botanic Gardens, Kew, 2nd edition*. Royal Botanic Gardens, Kew.

Farjon, Aljos. (2017). *Ancient Oaks in the English Landscape*. Royal Botanic Gardens, Kew.

Flanagan, Mark and Kirkham, Tony. (2009). *Wilson's China: A century on*. Royal Botanic Gardens, Kew.

Flora: Inside the Secret Word of Plants. (2018). Dorling Kindersley in association with Kew.

Fry, Carolyn. (2017). *The Plant Hunters: The adventures of the world's greatest botanical explorers,* revised edition. Andre Deutsch.

Fry, Carolyn; Seddon, Sue and Vines, Gail. (2011). *The Last Great Plant Hunt: The story of Kew's Millennium Seed Bank*. Royal Botanic Gardens, Kew.

Fry, Carolyn. (2013). *Kew's Global Kitchen Cookbook*. Royal Botanic Gardens, Kew.

Griggs, Patricia. (2011). *Joseph Hooker: Botanical trailblazer*. Royal Botanic Gardens, Kew.

Harrison, Christina. (2019). *Kew's Big Trees,* 2nd edition. Royal Botanic Gardens, Kew.

Harrison, Christina and Gardiner, Lauren. (2016). *Bizarre Botany*. Royal Botanic Gardens, Kew.

Harrison, Christina and Kirkham, Tony. (2019). *Remarkable Trees*. Thames & Hudson in association with Kew.

Harrison, Christina; Rix, Martyn and Yamanaka, Masumi. (2015). *Treasured Trees*. Royal Botanic Gardens, Kew.

Mills, Christopher (ed.) (2016). *The Botanical Treasury.* Andre Deutsch in association with Kew.

North, Marianne. (2018). *Marianne North: The Kew Collection*. Royal Botanic Gardens, Kew.

Parker, Lynn and Ross-Jones, Kiri. (2013). *The Story of Kew Gardens in Photographs*. Arcturus Publishing.

Payne, Michelle. (2018). *The Temperate House*. Royal Botanic Gardens, Kew.

Payne, Michelle. (2016). *Marianne North: A very intrepid painter, 2nd edition*. Royal Botanic Gardens, Kew.

Price, Katherine. (2017). *Get Plants: how to bring green into your life*. Royal Botanic Gardens, Kew.

Scott, Katie; Gaya, Ester; Hawksworth, David L.; Suz, Laura M.; Kooij, Pepijn W.; Liimatainen, Kare; Prescott, Tom and Davies, Lee. (2019). *Fungarium*. Big Picture Press in association with Kew.

Sherwood, Shirley. (2019). *The Shirley Sherwood Collection: Masterpieces of botanical art*. Royal Botanic Gardens, Kew.

Sherwood, Shirley and Rix, Martyn. (2008). *Treasures of Botanical Art*. Royal Botanic Gardens, Kew.

Walker, Kim and Nesbitt, Mark. (2019). *Just the Tonic: a natural history of tonic water*. Royal Botanic Gardens, Kew.

Wilford, Richard. (2016). *The Great Broad Walk Borders*. Royal Botanic Gardens, Kew.

Willis, Kathy and Fry, Carolyn. (2014). *Plants from Roots to Riches*. John Murray.

Willis, Kathy and Scott, Katie. (2016). *Botanicum*. Big Picture Press in association with Kew.

ACKNOWLEDGEMENTS

All photography by Jeff Eden, Paul Little and Andrew McRobb except where specified below.

We would like to thank the following for providing photographs and for permission to reproduce copyright material: Cover: front and back, Jeff Eden, Inside: John Millar; Tomás del Amo; Hina Joshi; Jean Postle; Tiziana Ulian; Wolfgang Stuppy; Wilkinson Eyre Architects; Marks Barfield Architects; Walters & Cohen Architects; John Pawson Ltd; Skyvantage; Historic Royal Palaces.

Thank you to the following for their valued help and advice with this edition: Richard Barley, Julia Buckley, Lorna Cahill, Janine Durkin, Joanna Ellams, Aljos Farjon, Gina Fullerlove, Richard Gianfrancesco, Tony Hall, Christina Harrison, David Holroyd, Tony Kirkham, Carlos Magdalena, Christopher Mills, Mark Nesbitt, Justine Parker, Michelle Payne, Andre Schuiteman, Rhian Smith, Lydia White, Richard Wilford, Colin Ziegler.

INDEX

Reprinted with revisions in 2017, 2018, 2019, 2020
First published in 2014
Royal Botanic Gardens, Kew, Richmond, Surrey, TW9 3AE, UK
www.kew.org

ISBN 978 1 84246 504 2

Distributed on behalf of the Royal Botanic Gardens, Kew in
North America by the University of Chicago Press,
1427 East 60th Street, Chicago, IL 60637, USA.

British Library Cataloguing in Publication Data
A catalogue record for this book is available from the British Library.

Text: Katherine Price
Design, typesetting and page layout: Jeff Eden and Christine Beard
Project and production management: Georgina Hills
Revisions: Christina Harrison and Gina Fullerlove
Front and back cover photographs: Jeff Eden

For information or to purchase all Kew titles, please visit shop.kew.org
or email publishing@kew.org

Kew's mission is to be the global resource in plant and fungal knowledge
and the world's leading botanic garden.

Kew receives approximately one third of its funding from Government
through the Department for Environment, Food and Rural Affairs
(Defra). All other funding needed to support Kew's vital work comes
from members, foundations, donors and commercial activities,
including book sales.

Printed and bound in Italy by Printer Trento srl.
Holder of the following quality, printing and environmental certifications: ISO 12647-
2:2004, Fogra® PSO (Process Standard Offset), CERTIprint®, ISO 14001:2004,
FSC®(C015829), Carbon Trust Standard.